# SELL MORE TOURS

## MATTHEW NEWTON

Copyright 2015.

# WARNING:

## DON'T MISS OUT ON THE FREE UPDATES TO THIS BOOK

More tips and tricks will be added to later editions of this book. I'll email you the new chapters for free as they are added! Visit [tourismtiger.com/bookupdates/](tourismtiger.com/bookupdates/)

I'll also be releasing FREE video tutorials about how to implement many of the techniques described in this book at the same URL: [tourismtiger.com/bookupdates/](tourismtiger.com/bookupdates/)

Do it now so you don't forget!

# Contents

PART 1: 7 FOUNDATIONS OF YOUR SUCCESS ............1

PART 2: TIPS TO SUCCEED WITH SOCIAL
MEDIA AND TRIPADVISOR ................................21

PART 3: EMAIL MARKETING & MARKETING
AUTOMATION ......................................................69

PART 4: A BASIC GUIDE TO OPTIMIZING
YOUR SITE FOR GOOGLE ...................................87

PART 5: GETTING LINKS TO YOUR SITE AND
BUILDING YOUR WEB PRESENCE...................123

PART 6: HOW TO CRUSH IT WITH VIDEO .....................143

PART 7: HOW TO MAKE PAID ONLINE
MARKETING WORK FOR YOU .........................157

PART 8: TURNING YOUR WEBSITE INTO
A SALES MACHINE ............................................185

PART 9: DELIVERING YOUR TOUR WITH
MARKETING IN MIND .......................................257

PART 10: RELATIONSHIPS & PARTNERSHIPS ...............275

PART 11: BONUS TIPS .......................................................293

# INTRODUCTION

This book has a lot of information in it. It's not a 'one idea' business book which can be read in one sitting (but if you do somehow manage it in one sitting, I applaud you!)

Instead, I would encourage you to view Sell More Tours as a reference book. See it as something where you only open up the relevant chapters and avoid feeling guilty because you jump the sections that are not relevant to you.

My mission is to help tourism focused businesses achieve effective marketing and if you follow the advice in this book, you will take a huge step towards having a sustainable, successful tourism business.

I've taken a huge amount of the knowledge acquired over my years of online marketing – for my own businesses and for clients all around the world – and laid it out for you here. If there's any new sections you'd like to see, email matthew@tourismtiger.com and I'll see what I can do to add that in.

The book has 11 parts:

Foundations of Your Success – I lay out 7 consistently important principles that you need to follow if you are to see basic sustained success in your business.

Tips to Succeed With Social Media and TripAdvisor – Social Media can mean a lot of wasted time if not done correctly. TripAdvisor is a tool that nearly all tour operators use at 50% of its potential and I want to show you a few extra ways to make sense of it.

Email Marketing and Marketing Automation – What emails should you be sending? When should you send them? How do you get people to give you their email to begin marketing to them? How can you do this effectively without annoying people? I get a lot of these questions and I've wrapped a lot of it up right here for you.

A Basic Guide to Optimizing Your Site for Google – SEO is a complex and confusing topic. I break it down for you by explaining Google's foundations, how Google works, how to engage in keyword research, what various terms mean, and what you actually need to focus on for optimizing your site.

Getting Links to Your Site and Building Your Web Presence – Building links still matters, but your overall web presence should be the primary focus. I share with you a lot of ideas for getting new links to your website in a systematic way, building off the work of your competition.

How to Crush it With Video – Video is increasingly important as a marketing tool and you need to start paying attention to it. I break down how to make great videos for your own site and how to start a Youtube channel which succeeds.

How to Make Paid Online Marketing Work for You – I've lost count of the amount of small business owners who I meet who have tried Google Adwords and given up on it. Add to that the growing presence of Facebook and this space is growing increasingly complex.

<u>Turning Your Website Into a Sales Machine</u> – Getting visitors to your website is hard work, which means that each one needs to be treated as precious gold. This part is broken down into four sections:

Section A – Getting Images Right

Section B – Writing to Sell

Section C – Designing to Sell

Section D – Converting the Sale

<u>Delivering Your Tour With Marketing in Mind</u> – Congratulations. You've done it! You've got a guest with you. Every step of your interaction with this guest needs to happen with your marketing in mind – from avoiding bad reviews to getting the guest to sign up for more tours.

<u>Relationships and Partnerships</u> – Who can you partner with to sell more tours? Accommodation is one big source. What about bloggers? I share with you a few small ideas to help you build the relationships needed to drive steady streams of referrals to your business.

<u>Bonus Tips</u> – A small grab bag of miscellaneous tips to round out your reading experience.

You are free to use the tips and strategies however you like. Pass it onto your marketing intern and tell them to go crazy.

Enjoy it and if you have any feedback – or spot any mistakes – let me know.

# PART 1

# 7 FOUNDATIONS OF YOUR SUCCESS

## Foundation 1: Keeping The People Around You Happy Is More Important Than Keeping Your Money

Nothing is more important for success than making sure that everyone who interacts with you comes away happy. Often it's the difference between success and failure. A happiness-focused owner enjoys torrents of repeat and referral business. Over time, they can reduce their dependence on first-time visitors. The opposite of a happiness-focused owner is not someone who has a mission to make people unhappy. They're just not being proactive about making people happy.

Right now, that could be you. Most mistakes in business not deliberate – they're accidental. If people leave unhappy, it could be there's something that you're overlooking without knowing.

We get the idea of making people happy intuitively when it comes to our guests, but did you know this is even MORE important for your staff?

Your staff will treat your guests more or less exactly how you treat them. If you do have staff, your #1 purpose in life needs to be <u>making their life great.</u>

Do you bend over backwards to make sure your guides are well equipped? Trained? Well paid? Rested? Empowered to make decisions without having to ask you? Happy?

I've talked to business people who complain that they 'find it so hard to get great people.' This is nonsense. Your staff are more or less a direct reflection of you. They are the most honest mirror you can ever hope to look into.

Do you have a genuine, beating desire to be the best boss they ever had? The proof is that your staff tell you!

Your guests can feed off the energy you and your staff send out. One sharp word can reduce an entire experience into nothing.

A single moment of bloody-minded inflexibility is all it takes to destroy your ranking on TripAdvisor.

One of the biggest causes of negative reviews is where the operator refuses to take responsibility for things out of their control. This puts it onto the guest's shoulders and ultimately their staff who have to deal with an unhappy guest.

Do companies with over a thousand 5-Star Reviews and just one or two 1-Star Reviews achieve this by accident? Their cars never break down, they never have rainy days, their guides never get sick, they never arrive at a restaurant which sends out bad food from the kitchen?

These businesses put aside short term profits in favor of a bigger vision.

It's easier said than done, and if you haven't laid out a plan to ensure this is the case you're going to get hurt at some point.

Basic causes of employee unhappiness:

1. Lack of training and processes. If someone makes a mistake in your business, it could well be your fault. Think about it – could the issue be for lack of process or training? Take responsibility for your employee errors – if you know how to do it, why don't they? There's only one person who can wear the blame for that.

2. Lack of trust and empowerment, where even the best-hearted people can go wrong. People HATE working for worriers, even if they are great people when they take off their 'boss' hat. Let go and trust your employees. Give them the independence to make decisions up to a certain value ($500, $1500) without having to consult you. Allow them to figure out their own way to solve problems. This last point is where I trip up most as a boss.

3. Lack of perceived fairness in policies. If your employees feel that your policies are unfair, they will never respect you as much as they could. They hate being in a position where they have to explain to the customer why they can't get a refund on their cancellation.

Most policies in a business have one purpose: to protect the business. This is counter-productive. Design your policies to protect your employees and customers. Stop worrying about small hits to your petty cash and think about the long term.

4. Lack of feedback and praise. You might love your employees but do they know it? Maybe you have a hectic business where you don't have much time to breathe. I get that. We have super busy times and I understand. You just need to be mindful of this and show your appreciation of your staff on a much more regular basis than you might

think. If you work hand in hand, I'm talking several times a day. Compliment them in front of your guests. Praise them on your social feed and on your website. Even if you don't work happen to work alongside them, always be looking for opportunities to encourage.

5. The owner doesn't take responsibility for things that happen outside their control. Just because it's not your fault doesn't mean it's not your responsibility to fix. Do everything to make things right for your clients. Be the happiness champion of your business.

Be proactive in making sure your guests and staff are happy. You may not become a millionaire overnight, but you have just set a wonderful foundation.

## FOUNDATION 2: KNOW WHAT MAKES YOU DIFFERENT AND PUSH IT EVERYWHERE

What makes you different? What gives people a reason to choose your particular trip over the next operator's? In marketing lingo, your special difference is known as your Unique Selling Proposition (or USP). It's a concept most know of but few fully understand.

A lot of operators focus solely on the product they're selling in their advertising. "Visit the Ryan Falls!" they'll say, while 5 other operators are saying the exact same thing.

If someone were to ask your typical customer why they chose you, what words would they use? That's your point of difference to that person.

"Oh, I went with the cheapest one."

"They have some really interesting tours."

"I chose the one that has the lunch included."

"They all seemed the same to me so I just picked randomly."

"I like that they have multiple tours – less hassle."

"I went with this woman who seems to have a few secret 'ins' around the area."

"My mum is disabled and I went with the only company that could take her wheelchair."

"I don't know. Bob just seemed nice."

Without a clear point of difference, you could well have great success but it will be more difficult. When people ask their hotel or hostel reception for a recommendation, do you spring to their mind? Or, is the hotel receptionist getting 4 brochures out and saying "well, they're all more or less the same..."

Having an obvious point of difference is one of the biggest keys to avoiding 'race to the bottom' price wars.

The easiest way to create a unique point of difference is to have a unique product. Segway tour companies are a perfect example of offering a completely different experience. While Segways are definitely awesome, you don't need to go that far. Think about not just your product but what makes your business inherently special.

Segways are also a weakness because your unique difference is out of your control – someone else could create an imitator.

Take the example of Hidden Secrets Tours, a walking tour company in Melbourne, Australia. From all external appearances they seem to be going well and have glowing reviews across social media.

They could have called themselves something boring like "Jade's Melbourne Walking Tours." Just having a name like "Hidden Secrets" draws me in and explains their point of difference in seconds. They seem like experts who will show me interesting places that I would never have found on my own. Sign me up now!

The result? They have a high ranking on TripAdvisor and are swimming. You may be wondering – did this give them the ability to avoid price wars? Heck yes it did! Their tours are not cheap! This is the difference a great Point of Difference can make!

## Foundation 3: People Look To Be With Their Herd. Know Your Ideal Customer And Speak Directly To Them

One of the biggest sins of marketing is being generic. While having a clear point of difference is the first step to avoiding this, the second step is knowing exactly who you are selling to. From there, you focus every aspect of your marketing energy around that target audience.

Operators who go for 18-25 year olds seem to get this best. They have photos of their guests having a crazy time and use edgy fonts all over their marketing. Guess what happens next? They get bookings from 18-25 year-olds! People will take their cues as to whether your tour is for them from the photos they see of other people on the same tour.

I was looking at the website of an Italian hiking guide recently. All the photos and testimonials showed him with outdoorsy 45-60 year-olds, which demonstrated perfectly who was his target client.

He didn't fall into the trap of trying to appear 'youthy' with photos of 25-35 year old young things plastered all over his site. He'd probably have a lot of difficulty getting many of those 50-60 year olds who are his bread and butter! Sure, I wouldn't personally book with the company – I've still got a ways to go to fit in with his herd– but that doesn't matter. If he chose to focus on no one, who would have been keen to book with him? No one.

The three steps to targeting your herd:

1. Ask yourself: what do members of your herd look like? If you offer physical activities, sometimes people will shy away from them because they think the tour is for exercise nuts, most especially if all your advertising is full of photos of fit young people. One tour operator I was working with had this exact problem. He would get a lot of questions about whether his mountain biking days were too strenuous for children or middle-aged people. The solution? Put up a photo right in the center on his website of a middle-aged guest enjoying the tour with their child. A picture speaks a thousand words.

2. Describe your true ideal customer in extreme detail. Think about the guest that without fail LOVES your company and fits perfectly with what you're doing. Who is that person? Write a profile out. How old are they? Where are they from? What do they like doing? How do they make buying decisions? What are their fears when traveling? What social network do they use? What do they do when they're not with you? What's their occupation?

3. Write all of your marketing copy directly to that person and use imagery that would appeal to them. Avoid the mistake of addressing your words to an unspecified group. Groups of people don't read your website or your brochure – individuals do. All of your marketing copy should be written as if you were writing directly to that individual. Imagine you were physically writing a message on Facebook to that person. You'd do it a bit differently than if you were using typical boring corporate speak.

You should notice an uptick in business from the category

you are targeting. It's part of your point of difference as a company and will save you time AND generate more sales.

Knowing your herd guides you in everything, not just the photos you put on your site. If you are targeting a 40-50 year old market who tends to like small group experiences, I doubt you will waste much time building relationships with youth hostels or business focused hotel groups. Naturally, what you'd be doing is trying to build relationships with business owners who in and of themselves fit your target market, because they will be able to see your value proposition better than anyone.

## FOUNDATION 4: HOW TO GET MASSIVE MOMENTUM FROM TINY ACTIONS IN YOUR TOURISM BUSINESS

"We are what we repeatedly do. Excellence, then, is not an act, but a habit." - Aristotle

Marketing isn't a thing you sit down to do every now and then and then BOOM... radiant success! Continuous action is what will drive you forward. Lots of small steps one after the other. Monday - action. Tuesday - action. Wednesday – action.

Every single day, one small step. Make this your motto and you will succeed.

A classic logical mistake is that we overestimate what we can do in the short-term but underestimate what we can do in the long-term. You can do amazing things just by grinding out actions every single day! It's like when you climb a mountain and turn around to look down – you feel amazed at what you've just accomplished. You're so high up yet all you did was plonk one foot after the other.

If you improve by 50% every year, what would this mean to you within a few years? Dedicate yourself to your craft and to marketing it. Carve time out of your schedule and make growing your business the first thing you focus on every single day. The first two hours of my day are always dedicated to growing my business. I don't check emails or do ANYTHING besides move forward. This is how it should be.

Here's a few steps to make this happen:

1. Define the high level activities you need to undertake. Responding to client emails is not one of them. You do need to respond to your customer emails at some point in the day but in this case we're talking about things that increase your presence and mind-share. Doing social media or sending emails to fellow tourism business owners is a great step. Try to step out of the hum-drum of everyday activities and focus on bigger things.

2. Block out a time every day to conduct these activities. This is the key - stick to it harder than a fanatic. No excuses are acceptable. Make it the first thing you do every day and you'll find it a lot easier to maintain the habit.

3. Measure the activities using goals and numbers. In my business, we sit down and track every single Monday how many followers we have added on Facebook, Twitter and LinkedIn the previous week. In fact, we review around 20 different numbers in our weekly team meeting with a particular focus on actionable metrics over vanity metrics. We'll talk more about this later in the book.

You could even have a goal of sending 1 email each day to someone in your network. Remember the famous saying – what gets measured gets done.

4. Wait four years and buy yourself a yacht.

## Foundation 5: The Know-Like-Trust Principle

Most Tour Operators depend on this principle, aware of it or not. For a business to be an effective customer-winning machine, you need to get people to know you, like you and trust you.

This simple rule can guide all of your marketing and turn yourself from a johnny-also-ran into a johnny-just-paid-off-his-house-early.

Here's the three things you need to achieve to get that booking:

1. Know you: getting people to hear about you in the first place via brochures, your website, TripAdvisor or any other form of marketing.

2. Like you: engage with the personality of you the owner, and the personality of your brand. The idea here is to steer clear of the typical corporate-speak that emanates from large companies. You don't need to be a clown - you just need to show a bit of who you are and not hide behind logos.

3. Trust you: Show them the proof as to why you're a great operator and why they should take the risk of spending their money on your business. Awards, number of tours, media mentions.

Beyond your own marketing, the K-L-T principle is why referrals work so well - all of that relationship capital gets transferred from one person to the next.

It explains why TripAdvisor has been so successful for so many businesses. You can receive all that trust that comes from the TripAdvisor brand.

This principle also explains why it can be so painful to sell to strangers who have never heard of you outside of train stations or at boat docks. You'll now see why it's so difficult – you simply haven't taken them through the K-L-T process.

All the copy and photos on your website need to use this idea. Are you showing people why they should trust you? Does your business seem like a cardboard cut-out or does it have likable personality?

## Foundation 6: Know Your Numbers Up And Down

What's your margin per head? How many spots do you need to sell on each tour to break even – both gross and net margins? How much money does each marketing channel cost you per landed booking?

It's impossible to run a great business without first getting your numbers in place and knowing them down to the ground.

How do you know if you even have the right price on your tour if you don't know exact costs and profits associated with your entire business? If you don't know your per-head margin and break-even figures, it will be hard to optimize for future cash-flow.

On The Shark Tank or The Profit (two shows I love), you'll notice they will heavily judge an entrepreneur who doesn't know their numbers. It's your ticket to legitimacy as a business person and I don't say this lightly.

Profit is the money left over after all expenses. You know this. By knowing your numbers, you know exactly which levers to pull to generate more of that profit. Many people who rubbish Adwords are the exact people who don't know their numbers (a generalization here, but bear with me). Tracking the effect of Adwords is fairly difficult and requires an expert – either internal or a consultant – to set things up to track the effect.

In 2013, I worked with someone who had just stopped

Adwords because they thought they were losing money on it. They hadn't even set up tracking so they had no way of knowing if they were making a profit on it. Once I did the analysis, we saw that their previous month had generated around $100 of revenue for every $16 spent!

Taking the opposite side, a while back I consulted for a business where the partners were fighting amongst themselves. It was a terrible situation where the business was losing money with no real hope of recovery. They were spending around $5000 a month on Adwords and one of the partners was convinced that they had to keep going. Once I looked at the numbers I was able to show that Adwords was generating – you will not believe this – just $460 on average per month in revenue. Terrible. If you don't have a method for tracking the return of spend on marketing, you'll be lucky to stay in business going into the future. All around you, your competition is growing sharper and more refined.

Let's have a look at some steps you can take to improve your numbers:

1. Set up Google Analytics tracking the right way. You can install Google Analytics yourself but to configure it correctly you need to take extra steps and this should be done by an expert. It's possible, for example, to show which marketing sources are leading to questions through your contact form. Facebook may be generating traffic but is it generating customers? We can show this kind of thing in Google Analytics when configured correctly.

2. You need to be tracking all numbers in a spreadsheet on an ongoing basis and have the capability to track changes

over time. Numbers mean nothing without context. Being able to compare year on year performance is invaluable.

3. Be mindful of the cost of time. Facebook is 'free' to post on, but time-sucking. Sending employees around the streets with leaflets can actually be a good idea but make sure to track the cost of their time in doing so. Not just the hourly rate you pay them, but their entire cost to you as an employee.

4. Make sure you have a great bookkeeper or accountant who is engaged with your business and understands what is needed to take you to the next level.

5. Get your team on board. Business owners who keep numbers to themselves are the majority but it's not clever. You'll be surprised just how fully employees will become part of your mission if you just allow them to be. If they can see the breakdowns of expenses and the movements in performance, you're much more likely to get them on board with you. Why? Because now they understand the context! It's all too easy to think poorly of your team but if they are operating in an information vacuum what can you expect from them?

6. Focus on actionable metrics instead of vanity metrics. Vanity metrics are things like number of website visitors or number of Facebook followers. Things like website conversion rate, Facebook post engagement and percentage of repeat business have more effect on your success. As a result, they should be tracked more closely.

## Foundation 7: The Three Channels Principle

You may find this book overwhelming at points because we'll be covering many topics. In fact, you may well find yourself with a large to-do list and feeling stressed about it all.

That's why you need to be aware of the Three Channels Principle. The idea is that you should be focused on crushing it on no more than three marketing channels at any given moment.

You've probably found yourself pulled in a million directions – Facebook! Twitter! Instagram! Send flyers to hotels! Go to conferences! Blog! Youtube! Vehicle signage! PR!

If you work on any more than three at one time, you will struggle to focus and find it super tough to execute effectively on any of them. Avoid the shotgun approach. For any marketing channel to work, you'll need to give a lot of thought and attention to how you're doing it.

By building a foundation first you'll greatly enhance the chances of that channel succeeding for you. This could mean spending a lot of time researching TripAdvisor and evaluating your own strategy.

Move on and begin to focus on other channels once you have that foundation installed and you have a working system in place. You may never even want to move on if those three channels are having great success for you. Just know that you can never judge a marketing channel with a half-hearted effort.

This is what makes marketing so difficult – you often won't know if a certain tactic works for you without 6 months of consistent work. Sounds like a sure recipe for wasted time, right? I disagree. Everything you do in marketing sharpens your skills.

# PART 2

# TIPS TO SUCCEED WITH SOCIAL MEDIA AND TRIPADVISOR

## How TripAdvisor's Ranking System Works

"How can I increase my rankings in TripAdvisor?" If I had a one dollar coin for every time someone asked me that question, I could buy lots of mint chocolate chip ice cream (I really, really like ice cream).

Here's the answer: Understand what TripAdvisor wants and give it to them. When you give TripAdvisor what they want, they will return the favor (hopefully!)

So what does TripAdvisor actually want? Let's start with the obvious - the #1 thing that TripAdvisor wants is more profits.

TA's profits come from having active users - when they have active users, they make money. Their stock market valuation goes up and down based on how many active users they have – it's a big deal! In fact, 'active users' is one of the key metrics for all social media websites including Facebook, Twitter and Pinterest.

Because of this, there's a lot of pressure on the CEO of TripAdvisor to get and keep more active users. Keep the CEO happy!

There's two ways for TripAdvisor to get an active user - sign up a completely new user or convert a currently inactive user into an active user.

Following on from active users, the #2 thing that TripAdvisor wants is useful information. If a user is on their website but clicks away, that person is lost. To keep them, TripAdvisor needs valuable content!

This means that TripAdvisor will reward you for keeping their users active and getting them to post content.

Here are the three main ranking factors on TripAdvisor for Tour Operators, according to them:

1. Average review score (far and away the most important!)

2. Quantity of reviews

3. Recency of reviews

This is important to understand: TripAdvisor will reward you for keeping their users active and happy. So, what do you need? A steady stream of positive reviews. Obviously, these are not the ONLY three factors in the TripAdvisor algorithm – as anyone who has ever analyzed the TA rankings will know. However, they're the major three.

Do you have a system for generating more reviews? Many operators don't. Your TripAdvisor rankings - and thereby, a potential large source of your revenue – depends on it. Their statistics show that listings with 10+ reviews receive 26% more engagement, so – clearly - they are going to reward that.

Before I finish, you may be aware of certain websites which have been engaging in conspiracy theories about TripAdvisor. Please don't listen to them. While they are able to show some strange movements in the TripAdvisor algorithm, what can you do about it? It's a computer. Of course it will throw out strange results from time to time. Avoid the whiners, stay focused on doing a great job and you'll win eventually as TA's systems become more refined.

Buying advertising won't help your rankings, either. It's actually illegal in the USA for a website to change its rankings in a paid way without disclosure and this is something that the FTC polices strictly. If you're thinking of engaging in paid advertising on TripAdvisor, only do it if the actual spend makes sense for your business.

## AFTER THE TRIP, GET THAT TRIPADVISOR REVIEW, STAT

As you'd know, TripAdvisor doesn't allow you to offer incentives to get reviews. As much as they want active users, people won't stay active for long if one can't depend on the information and reviews provided on their website.

What you can do, however, is follow up with an email just thanking your guest for coming along and asking for a review at the same time. That's not so hard.

If you follow up with photos of their trip in that email, this will work even better for you. Because they have just received a bunch of photos they have a reason to be grateful. This is more or less as far as you can push it when it comes to more TripAdvisor reviews, but it's perfectly fine. Just make sure not to present the delivery of the photos as something you did in exchange for a review.

Deliver the photos and at the end of the email say 'if you had a great time, could you leave us a review? Our business depends on the 5 star reviews we receive. Thank-you!'

The great thing is if you upload the photos to Facebook as part of your process, you can include a link to your Facebook page in the automatic email that comes out to them after the trip. This is a capability that most tour booking software operators provide which means you can execute this process without any additional work.

When should you send the email? Now that people check their email more or less every day, I'd recommend sending it as soon as possible after the tour so their great memories with you are still fresh and front of mind.

# How To Get More Reviews Automatically With No Extra Work

This is one of the shortest chapters in the book, yet one of the most powerful.

There's a good chance you want to dominate the TripAdvisor rankings. Good news: right here you'll find the secret behind nearly every tour operator in the top 10 all over the world. If you don't believe me, close the book after reading this chapter and go check for yourself! The people holding #1 right now hate that I'm sharing this because they don't want anyone else to know this simple information.

So, what's the goose that lays the golden egg? Right here:

1. Take online bookings using a specialist tour operator booking software system.

2. Schedule follow-up emails for bookings to ask them for a review (as per the previous chapter).

The automated nature means that you have a steady stream of reviews trickling each week. TripAdvisor gets what they want – more active users – and you get what YOU want – higher rankings.

If you don't have a modern website with a real-time booking option available to potential customers, close this book and please do it now. Don't let another day slip by. If you already have a booking system, ?schedule the emails!? Nearly all online tour software services give you this option. Make use of it and see your profits rise.

How should you do it?

Alex Bainbridge of TourCMS states:

"Use a subject line such as "welcome home" rather than anything to do with feedback. These two changes alone increased response to one tour operators welcome home email by 200-300%."

This is excellent advice!

# How To Respond To TripAdvisor Reviews To Get More Bookings

First things first: you are replying to all TripAdvisor (and Yelp) reviews, right? I hope you are.

In fact, it's a good idea to make it an every day habit to respond to your reviews. A few of you might wonder if you should even reply at all to reviews. Does it actually help or is it just a waste of time? Here's the answer: in a user survey conducted by PhoCusWright, one of the results was this: "57% of users agreed that seeing hotel management responses to reviews generally makes me more likely to book it." I don't think it's too much of a leap to suggest that this is also relevant to tour operators.

Other statistics, from TripAdvisor:

- 77% of respondents said that seeing a hotel Management Response makes them believe that the hotel cares more about its guests.

- 62% said that seeing management responses makes them more likely to book with them

We'll deal with negative reviews in a second but let's get to some general principles.

How should one respond to a review? To know the answer to this, we need to consider WHY we are responding to reviews. A lot of tour operators respond to reviews without taking the time to think "why am I actually doing this?"

The primary goal of responding to a review is to help you get bookings. Will you get more? Sure – TripAdvisor's own statistics show that listings with 50% of reviews responded to are 24% more likely to receive an inquiry!

The secondary goal of responding to a review is make whoever is reading want to keep on reading. We shouldn't be responding to reviews just for the sake of it.

There's three basic rules to achieve this:

Keep it Informal

Keep it Short

Keep it Personal

Make your response read like a personal email you would send in private.

It's amazing how many people screw this one up. I've looked at hundreds of profiles on TripAdvisor and maybe 5-10% of tour operators get this right.

What are people looking for when they read responses? Why would they read it? They're looking to see if you are a likable person. This means you'll get more bookings if people can see that your guests make a personal connection with your business.

Here's how to achieve that:

1. Be casual. Taking your marketing cues from the pages of the AT&T Manual for Customer Service is not clever, yet so many do it!

I find the advice on the internet about 'how to respond to reviews' to be inadequate. Avoid those formal, corporate sounding replies that no one would ever want to read yet which so many are telling you to write. Use your reply to show a bit of PERSONALITY (unless you actually enjoy boring people!)

The below example (edited to make it anonymous) is what I mean. It might seem fine to you but stop for a second here - what is the business owner actually saying? It's nothing besides empty words. Dragging your words straight out of Corporate Customer Service 101 is not going to help you get more bookings.

"Thanks so much for your review. I'm delighted you found that booking our tour was the right decision and you and your family had such a good time. We trust you will all enjoy the rest of your travels here just as much! Thanks again for the feedback and choosing our tour.

Regards"

This is generic. How would this reply ever help an operator get more business?

2. Keep it Short and Sweet. Use as many words as necessary and not one more. Here's an example straight from TripAdvisor that did a decent job:

"Thank-you for taking the time to leave a review. Your family was a lot of fun. You were a champ! It was a pleasure showing you around."

3. Be Personal. Remember that people on holiday want to come home with precious memories. You may not think you're special but a lot of people get a real kick out of building a personal connection with their tour guide. The tour guide will often be the only local they ever meet! Show

that this could happen in your responses.

The above quoted response was good and gave a sense of personal connection but it still could have been better. It didn't mention personal details or a fun thing that happened on the trip.

This response, copied straight from TripAdvisor, is perfect:

"First review you have ever done I can see! Thank-you. Loved showing you around. Best wishes in your future together and thanks for letting me share part of your honeymoon with you :)"

4. Skip the Sales Pitch. Many Tour Operators wisely see responding to reviews as the opportunity it is to help sell their business. But that doesn't mean you should be outright selling your service in the MIDDLE of a personal response. Avoid any naked selling. As above, you 'sell' your tours in your response by showing real humanity, warmth, connection and personality.

This is an actual example of someone inserting a sales pitch into their response:

"I am especially pleased you enjoyed the food - we invest a significant amount of time into sourcing and maintaining the quality and value of this part of our service from our local suppliers."

People have a lot of reviews to read. If the first response they see from you is boring and pitchy, they won't read any more. Lose the sales stuff and show your human side – if your TripAdvisor responses are full of personality and warmth, they'll keep on reading them and you may just land the booking.

## How To Deal With Negative Reviews

Do you have a negative review you're struggling to respond to? Email us at help@tourismtiger.com and we'll review your response for free before you post it - regardless of whether you're a client or not.

If you're getting a ton of negative reviews, nothing will save you (well, on TripAdvisor at least.)

Yet, if you get only the occasional negative review, people will look to your response to see whether the review was fair or not.

If there's 90 good reviews and 1 bad review, people will obviously give you a chance to explain yourself. The proof, from PhoCusWright: "84% of users agree that an appropriate management response to a bad review "improves my impression of the hotel" while "64% of users agree that an aggressive/defensive management response to a bad review "makes me less likely to book that hotel".

The basic goal of responding to a negative review is to come across as a relaxed, friendly person. It's a bit like a political debate – if one person is angry and aggressive and the other person is friendly, measured and calm, that second person will generally win. The tone of your response is ever so crucial.

There's three types of negative reviews: the generic 'I didn't enjoy it', the specific but completely wrong 'they didn't even bring me water!' kind of reviews and the specific but seemingly accurate ones such as 'they used a replacement guide without warning us and he was unfriendly.' Each requires its own type of response.

Here's a few simple tips for dealing with negative reviews the right way:

1. Take a Moment. Getting negative reviews is something that ticks most people off, especially where it's unjust. Don't respond straight away. Put it aside for an hour or two and let your thoughts circulate.

2. REALLY Take a Moment. It's too easy to just dismiss negative reviewers as being idiots. The reality is that nearly all your negative reviews give you a GENUINE opportunity to improve. Most people – including negative reviewers – are honest and offer you a path to get better. This became apparent when our team conducted an analysis of negative reviews in Melbourne, Australia.

A disproportionate amount of negative reviews come when a tour operator makes a change to a tour that the guest wasn't expecting. They might switch in a different guide, take a different route or merge two tour groups at the last moment. All these situations could be improved upon by a tour operator and if not avoided, at least prepared for.

Take the time to investigate the issue but don't wait too long – you need to get a response up there ASAP!

3. Be Personal - Don't Use a Stock Answer. "We take all feedback seriously" is (nearly) always written by someone who doesn't actually take feedback seriously.

Get away from the clichés and stock responses. Do not use words that make you seem like a corporate PR department because that's a quick track to irrelevance.

4. Don't Snipe Back. Stay positive and don't forget that the whole world is reading. If you get upset, make attacks or start using identifying details you'll lose a whole bunch of customers you could have had.

This is an example from TripAdvisor of a response gone wrong. The customer said she had received a rude email from the owner and this was part of his reply:

"I'm disappointed your experience was not what you had hoped for and that you've mistaken my response as being rude and hostile."

Wow. Passive aggressive much? The response should have been:

"I'm honestly shattered that my email came across that way… I really wasn't trying to be rude or hostile. If you see the rest of the reviews you'll know that I put so much effort into making people happy. I've just sent you an another email, hopefully I can make this right for you."

5. Address the Issue Directly. State that you have investigated the issue (if it needed investigating) and what you have done to fix it.

Nearly all negative reviews that I see do raise genuine issues where a response is required. Show your genuine desire to improve by actually looking into matters raised and fixing the causes of the problem. Note: in this type of response, it is SO crucial that you use human language here. Use "looked into" instead of "investigated", "fixed" instead of "corrected".

6. Feel Free to Express Appropriate Emotion. Express the impact on you and that you're distraught that someone had a negative experience.

I'm not talking about aggressive emotion. The worst thing (obviously) is to get angry in your response but the second worst thing is a cardboard, impersonal reply.

Much better:

"Hey Joanne, we honestly thought you were enjoying yourself! This kind of thing matters really matters to us and I'm shattered to think you had a bad time."

This leads to our next step.

7. Make it Good. Where appropriate in your response, offer to make it up to them. Say that you'll do anything to make it right, and if you had just known at the time you would have done something about it.

It's tricky to say "if I had known at the time" without coming across as snarky. "If you had bothered to tell me…" is quite obviously not the best way to do it.

"We're always ready to make things good so I've just tried to get in touch with you to offer a refund if you need one. Please check your email."

8. Correct Them With Grace. From time to time, a negative review will be a bit malicious. They might say things which are completely incorrect or neglect to mention the real reason you kicked them off your boat.

You have to tread so carefully here. If you bite back, you won't look great to potential guests.

This is why you need to open with a line such as this:

"I've never been a fan of 'he-said she-said' situations, but given this review is public I feel the need to respond and help shed some light on what happened here."

By introducing it like this, you come across as someone who is graceful and has not lost their temper. Do everything you can to avoid getting emotional and come across as calm and in control.

You could have someone sit next to you and give them the mouse to click the 'submit' button. In this way, the reply only goes up when both of you are satisfied with it.

9. Don't Mention The Business Name. If people Google your business name, do you want the negative review to show up? This is why I recommend not using your business name in your responses. So don't say this:

"On behalf of the team at Sundowner Tours, we would like to..."

Doing so could put that negative review in front of more eye-balls than you'd like!

# TRACK AND GROW REVIEWS AS A TEAM

As a team, you all need to be aware of your ranking in TripAdvisor and the effect that reviews can have. Every single person working for your operation has a vested interest in seeing your business make more money as it gives them pride and job security.

Here are some suggestions to make this happen:

1. Have a definitive, stated goal as to the number of reviews you are targeting. Keep it realistic as you won't get 50% of your guests to leave you reviews no matter how hard you try.
2. Review all goals as a team on a regular basis. In your weekly or monthly team meeting, make sure that one item that is always on the agenda is the topic of TripAdvisor (and Yelp).
3. Reward the entire team when a goal is hit.
4. Read the reviews as a team and publicly praise staff members when they have done a great job.

If you take a helicopter view of your business and regularly take the time to improve the performance of your marketing, this will come naturally to you.

## Run Through Negative Reviews Of Other Businesses With Your Staff As Part Of Their Ongoing Training

Reading negative reviews of other tour operators is often an eye-opening learning experience.

Sit down with your staff regularly and browse TripAdvisor and Yelp for negative reviews – then try to come up with a plan together as to how you would have a) prevented the situation and b) rectified the situation.

Avoiding negative reviews is much more important than gaining good reviews just because of the massive impact they can have. Make sure all staff are on board with your customer service policies and have regular discussions about them. Make sure they are empowered to find solutions to problems and can break the rules if they feel it will resolve a situation favorably for your business.

At the start of the book I talked about the importance of treating your staff well and emphasized how this would flow onto customer service. Those words remain true, but you may find that from time to time staff will not deal well with an unhappy customer because they're trying to protect your business. By constantly talking about this and using TripAdvisor negative reviews as part of their training, you'll keep them on the same page as you in terms of what is the big picture for your business. Help them understand that refusing a refund could cost you a lot more in lost bookings from the negative review that follows.

# How To Nail Your TripAdvisor Profile

Besides reading reviews about your business on TripAdvisor, people will browse your profile. Is one extra sale worth it? Two?

1. Be descriptive in the business name. People should be able to get a basic impression of what you do just from the name of your profile. If it's 'Marta's Tours', you're missing out a bit here. 'Marta's Tours Jamaica' or 'Marta's Kingston Day Tours' is much more clear.

TripAdvisor restricts this practice to prevent people jamming their profile name with keywords for the sake of Google but it's worth trying.

2. In your description, make every word count. Skip the fluffy marketing sentences such as "Your time here is limited, so make the most of it!" or "We provide a personal service which is tailored to you". Have a quick summary sentence about what you do (including your point of difference) to hook them into reading the rest.

Most visitors to a place have no clue how to differentiate one tour operator from another. This is why TripAdvisor reviews can help so much. Use your description to help further that sense of being the 'safe choice'. In your opening sentence or two, make a reference to how many hundreds or thousands of tours you have conducted. Maybe say which year you launched to show your experience. Quote a testimonial. Show that you're the operator that a smart person would choose.

The key here is to think of hooks – what opening sentences will interest people more than others? I LOVE the way Broadway Up Close Walking Tours does this. They're a highly successful tour company in New York:

"Have you ever wanted to know which Broadway theaters are haunted? Are you curious to know what a Broadway 'swing' is? Have you ever heard about the ghost light? If so, then this tour is just for you!"

What a great way to open their description. You'll need to strike a neat balance of interesting hooks, showing why your business is great and description of the tour.

3. Fill out your profile with detail. One noticeable thing on TripAdvisor is that lesser-ranked operators often have near-empty profiles. This makes them look inactive, even when they're not! Fill all the boxes – email, website, phone number, address. Add as many photos as you can. Make it look like a lot is going on.

4. I repeat: add photos. Lots of them. Instead of fancy-dancy shots of the sun setting over the horizon, show guests having fun. According to TripAdvisor, travelers engage 150 percent more with pages that have 20 or more photos! Make sure you don't wait for people to add photos on their own. Get them happening yourself instead.

5. Use video. According to TripAdvisor, hotel profiles with videos receive 34% more engagement than those that don't. You can imagine that this flows on to day tours as well.

6. Keep the info up to date. This is often overlooked. Put an entry into your diary to check the info every 3 or 6 months. Change up your profile info and your photos to keep it

fresh.

7. Test all links and contacts. It's common to see that businesses have put an incorrect link to their website. They have no idea, but if they had tested it just once they would have known.

8. Keep Google in mind. It's possible that by doing this that you can help your own page in TripAdvisor get a good ranking and thereby more visits. I've helped clients to do it before - you just need to make sure that you don't destroy the readability of your profile! The priority here needs to be the reader first and not Google. Just take a look at your profile and see if you can't sneak a keyword or two in there to optimize for Google searches.

9. Integrate booking links where possible. TripAdvisor has a 'book now' button where people can book directly through your site. You need to consider whether this is right for your business. If you know your numbers, do the maths. An extra bump in sales might not be worth it if they start taking commissions from bookings you would have gotten anyway. To get this feature enabled, you need to be listed on one of TripAdvisor's partner sites, for example Viator.

10. Respond to all your reviews. Responding to reviews increases the chances of someone engaging with your TA page. In fact, a TripAdvisor study showed that accommodation venues that respond to 50 percent or more of reviews experience 24 percent more engagement! Another study showed that 77 percent of users agree that seeing a hotel management response makes them more likely to book. It's hard to imagine that this doesn't also

apply to other businesses.

**11. Link back to your profile from your social media.** If your TripAdvisor profile makes you look great, put links to it in your Facebook Page description or your Twitter profile. Potential guests can then see the wonderful job you have done.

**12. Use the words of happy visitors.** Open your TripAdvisor profile description with a single sentence quote from a testimonial (or two). It's a great hook to begin your description because most operators don't do this and are boring. Every time I see a quote at the start of a profile, I'm interested to keep on reading. Even if you don't want to open your description by quoting a testimonial, I strongly recommend quoting one or two somewhere.

## Embed The TripAdvisor Widget Somewhere On Your Site – Or Go To The Next Level

TripAdvisor offers no shortage of little widgets that you can embed on your site. I personally feel the TripAdvisor widget is more valuable and will get more clicks than the 'Certificate of Excellence' awards that people embed. But, if you have both, embed both even if it's just in the footer of your site. More important website real estate should be taken with higher priority elements.

Embedding widgets is one thing. Can you take it a step further? I personally don't pay much attention to widgets except to see the ranking on TripAdvisor of a particular business. I know I definitely ignore the reviews listed in the widget, so one thing I advise people to do is to copy TripAdvisor reviews across to their websites and insert them into the general flow of the content, where they are more likely to get read.

At the end of the review you can put a link to the actual review saying "Read Review on TripAdvisor," so people can see that it came from a legitimate trustworthy source.

We'll get into a lot more detail about testimonials later in the book. Testimonials are incredibly powerful (as you may have guessed), but there's ways to make them even MORE powerful.

## BE CAREFUL OF THE TRIPADVISOR CRACK

If you're doing amazing on TripAdvisor, that's great. It's also risky for you because it's a potential trap. If a massive proportion of your bookings come from TripAdvisor, are you ready for the day when you drop down the rankings? You're not going to stay there forever - no one does and no one will.

At some point in the future, no matter how far it is in the future, something will happen. You may not even receive a negative review - more businesses will switch on to the value of having a process for generating extra reviews and could leave you in the dust. It's possible! There's a million reasons why you could lose your top 5 spot so don't assume that it's permanent (the same goes for your Google rankings).

The internet is full of people griping about how TripAdvisor killed their business which is just code for "I was overly dependent on them and now I'm paying the price."

Don't forget, everyone below you wants your spot. Imagine if today I were to go ask the people below you "Hey, do you want to be #1 on TripAdvisor?" How many do you think would say yes?

Work hard, get your rankings but do understand that it's dog eat dog stuff. One or two negative reviews that come out of nowhere can take you way down in the rankings and put your business on life support. You might annoy one group of people who all take the time to leave a negative review one by one, and find yourself at #10. (Yes, this does happen to tourism businesses - I've seen one that had to shut down just because of the impact of ONE super annoyed group.)

It's crucial to have other marketing channels pumping and working for you too. Get them cranking and create a nice mix.

## Hire Nice Staff: The Simple Key To Making Sure You Consistently Get 5 Stars

The clear, shining difference between companies that get 100% 5-star reviews and those that don't is friendliness. This means that your number one staff-hiring criterion needs to be to pick people who are just nice and – crucially - are able to maintain this in the heat of battle.

The fact is, if something goes wrong during a tour, nearly everyone will give you a chance to rectify this.

Negative reviews come not from when something bad happens, but from receiving a cold shoulder when they attempted to rectify the situation.

This doesn't just apply to tour operators. In Malcolm Gladwell's Blink, he showed us a study which was looking at which factors influence whether wa doctor will get sued. The finding was shocking: likeability is more important than competence to predict which doctor will get sued.

"The overwhelming number of people who suffer an injury due to the negligence of a doctor never file a malpractice suit at all. Patients don't file lawsuits because they've been harmed by shoddy medical care. Patients file lawsuits because they've been harmed by shoddy medical care – and something else happens to them."

Gladwell, in fact, tells us:

"What comes up again and again in malpractice cases is

that patients say they were rushed or ignored or treated poorly."

So, you can be incompetent but if you're nice, then it's largely okay. While this kind of information is a bit scary when talking about doctors, it shows how important this point is. The friendly, smiling person who takes people's complaints ends up the winner.

The proof that this pays off comes from the Library Hotel Collection, who have consistently dominated TripAdvisor. Talking to EyeForTravel.com, their VP of marketing Adele Gutman had this to say:

"The secret is our people. We hire happy people who love to be of service, and we train them and coach them to create a sense of pride in people pleasing.

"If you do your bit to help them develop their skills and give them all the tools, plus the freedom to use their imagination and creative problem solving skills, needed to make people happy, you will be inspired to see how far they are ready to go for guests."

## SOCIAL MEDIA: PICK ONE SOCIAL CHANNEL AND GO ALL IN

With the presence of so many social channels out there, it's tempting to feel like you have to give equal love to all of them. This is a mistake.

If you're going to do social, go all the way in on one channel and use it like crazy. Facebook will generally be the best option, followed by Instagram if you have a 18-30 kind of crowd.

Twitter will in nearly all cases be a waste of your time when it comes to generating direct bookings. The focus here should be on networking and brand building with people in your local area. As for Pinterest, nearly the entire audience there is female. Remember that the majority of booking decisions are made by women, so it's definitely worth having a think about, especially if you relate to this marketplace.

It is not a mistake to use various social channels regularly, don't get me wrong. The companies that have the most success on social, however, are those who go nuts building their presence on one channel. Dive deep! Connect with people. Login regularly. Talk to your followers. Interact. Engage.

<u>Automatic Social Cross-Posting Can Be Effective but is Dangerous</u>

Picking a social channel to nail doesn't mean you need to forget about all the rest of them!

Did you know you can post to Instagram and automatically have your post uploaded to Twitter? If you post an image to Instagram, you can have it automatically uploaded to your accounts pretty much anywhere.

A great many tour operators do this but it's a dangerous idea. While it may save you time, it will often remove you the hassle of having people actually, you know, follow you. When a Tweet is automatically sent to Facebook, it's nearly always completely obvious and feels very disconnected. How are your followers going to feel? How are people who are thinking of following you going to feel? They definitely won't feel like engaging with you, that's for sure.

At the least make sure to be aware of what each system will do to your post when it goes up and that you fit the formatting guidelines of those networks.

A good place to start with social media automation is IFTTT.com or Zapier.com. Both allow you to automatically post to multiple social media accounts by linking them together.

## GET LISTED ON YELP

Get on Yelp! So many Tour Operators ignore Yelp that it makes you wonder what they did to annoy people so bad.

Yelp is growing everywhere. While it is still most important in the USA, it is getting significant traction in many other countries.

Another advantage to getting listed on Yelp is that their listings often rank highly in Google for money-making keywords. You can piggy-back on their success just by having a free listing!

Yelp is kicking serious butt with 139 million visitors monthly - that's half of TripAdvisor!

Let's be honest here: most people on Yelp are looking for food and not tours. That doesn't mean that no one is looking for tours! Many people on Google are looking for saucy videos but that doesn't stop you from trying to get business there, does it?

Yelp will make a profile for you anyway.

Not convinced about Yelp? No worries! Yelp will make you a profile anyway using publicly available business data. It will look terrible, though.

How to Create a Yelp Listing That Makes Your Tourism Business Shine:

1. Claim Your Listing. This seems like a no brainer, but 40% of businesses on Yelp still haven't claimed their listing

2. <u>Spy on your competition.</u> Before making a listing on any site, you should always inspect the listings of other companies to find the best practices and then apply them to your own listing.

Not only that, but the reviews left on other profiles can give you a fantastic insight as to what other people are looking for when they go on tour.

As Brian Casel explains on Social Media Examiner: "Can you start to see patterns in the types of things mentioned in their reviews? Try to pin down what your local market values highly and what prompts them to leave a poor review."

3. <u>Delete the duplicates.</u> Before beginning on your profile, make 100% sure you don't have a listing created by Yelp or someone else.. Duplicate listings wil create a confusing mess for both you and your visitors.

4. <u>Complete the basics</u>

a. <u>Fill in all the boxes</u>. The emptier your profile, the less likely someone will call you.

Take business hours, as an example. Many tour operators don't put this in - why? If I can't see your business hours, I might assume your business has closed down! Putting your business hours gives people the security that they're calling at the right time and not interrupting you. It might be a small thing, but a great profile is all about the little details.

b. <u>Make sure your contact information is consistent</u> with your Google Plus page and your website. Inconsistent information confuses Google and leads to lower rankings.

c. Pick the right categories. For most operators, this will be 'tours.' Take advantage of additional categories, however, such as 'Bike Rentals', 'Ethnic Food' (for those doing food tours), 'Wine Tours', 'Transportation', 'Boat Charters' and more.

d. Write a great description. Write interesting and intriguing sentences. Quote your guests using testimonials. Break down what it is you do into bite-size points. The main thing you need to be concerned about is sounding boring and just talking about you, yourself, and your business. People aren't interested in that! Talk about what THEY want to hear.

For more thoughts on writing a great description, check out our post on creating a TripAdvisor profile that dominates right here - http://www.tourismtiger.com/blog/tour-operators-how-to-create-a-tripadvisor-profile-that-dominates/

4. Photos. Photos. Photos. Photos. Photos. Business listings with one photo receive 2.5x as much time per user . Upload photos from your guests or photos you take on tour. I'd recommend putting 20 at the very least. People never get tired of photos – Instagram and Facebook are great reminders of this.

5. Follow Your Followers. A clever tip that I found at the Fox Business site: follow your reviewers. Yelp tends to filter out reviews from 'orphan' accounts - those users that have signed up, left one review and done nothing else. By following these reviewers, there's a chance you might be able to get the review out of the filter.

6. Sell vouchers and/or gift certificates. Did you know that you can actually sell vouchers on Yelp? This means you can sell people a voucher for $40 off for $20. Yelp charges nothing to create these but will take a cut at the time of sale. It's a good way to motivate people to choose you over the next business.

At the time of writing, Yelp takes a cut of 30% for deals and 10% for gift certificates. It's not clear if this is available yet in all of the countries they serve.

7. Respond to ALL reviews. Responding to reviews creates an opportunity to build a human connection with your potential guests. Review responses that additional spark of interest and personality to every profile! In addition, it just makes people feel like you really care about the people who visit with you.

I was unable to find stats about Yelp, but on TripAdvisor we know that 62% of website visitors are more likely to book with businesses with management responses.

8. Respond to reviews the RIGHT way. There's many ways to respond to a review and most of them are simply wrong. Put simply, you're replying for the benefit of other people who visit the site - so make sure your responses make people want to check you out! Check out our chapters on TripAdvisor earlier in the book for more.

9. Track in Google Analytics. Do you have Google Analytics set up correctly with goals that match the function of your business? If not, you should!

Doing this, you'll have a great idea as to whether Yelp is helping you or not. This will help guide your decisions as to whether to dedicate more time or money to Yelp in the future.

10. Don't display their badges. Yelp will give you badges to display on your site. Honestly, I don't think they're worth showing, especially if you already have a TripAdvisor embed on your website.

Why? Your website will just get cluttered. The main thing you want is for people to book with you - once they're on your site, you shouldn't be pushing them away.

"But how do I take advantage of my amazing Yelp profile?"

Read point 11 :)

11. Quote your reviews on your website. If you're getting great reviews, you still want to showcase them right? Of course you do! One way to do this is just to copy the reviews across to your own site, pretty them up and put a link back to Yelp. While I'm sure they have something in their Terms and Conditions which says you can't do this... I'm sure it can't hurt.

12. Optimize your about this business page. In your truly excellent business description, consider doing a bit of light optimization for Google. I'm not saying you should spam your listing with keywords - bad idea! - rather that you should mention the aspects of your service which are the most searched for in general. This gives you a better opportunity at capitalizing on a bit of extra Google juice.

13. Don't offer incentives for reviews. Bribing people for reviews will just annoy Yelp. Don't risk your hard-earned status on Yelp by offering discounts or freebies to people. There's a good chance a competitor will catch you and

report you.

14. Read your reviews and act on them. There's no piece of information that tour operators are more inclined to ignore than a bad review. Let's face it - getting negative reviews sucks. Some reviewers might just be bad people but the majority are good people sharing actual experiences. Make use of that info.

15. Should you advertise on Yelp? Probably not. Take this with a big grain of salt, because each business is different. That being said, Yelp tries to lock their advertisers into long term contracts. There's only ONE reason a company does this - they know that advertisers wouldn't hang around after seeing the results. Personally, I find this very worrying and it's something that you won't find Google or Facebook doing.

Check out what marketing agency 39 Celsius had to say - "We decided to put Yelp ads on hold and put the budget into other more effective tactics, primarily Google Adwords."

## Encourage Your Guests To Post Images To Your Social

In the middle of a tour, grab people's cameras and take photos of them. Do selfies with your guests even! Get those photos and videos pumping and make your social media accounts a center of activity and laughs.

The key is to have fun! Take images with people that are fun, picturesque or even just plain funny.

Photos from your guests have much more power than the photos you take yourself on your own camera. They show that the people who come on your tour are genuinely having a great time and it gives potential visitors the longing to go there - or return.

What to do with these images:

1. Get Guests To Upload Them And Tag. There's any manner of places they can do so - Facebook, TripAdvisor, Instagram, Twitter, Pinterest. Same goes for videos. The options are almost limitless.

2. Upload Them Yourself to Social Media. Ask for your guest's perfmission, but you can then take a photo they have uploaded to Instagram and re-share it everywhere. I personally love it when companies share the photos taken by their customers. I doubt I'm alone in this.

3. Run Photo Competitions. You can upload 4 photos to Facebook and ask people to pick their favorite - the winner wins a $100 bottle of wine. Why not?

4. Use them on your website and other promo material. Again, be careful to ask for permission, but your guests will generate some incredible photos of themselves having fun which you can use to help sell your business. Most people will feel proud to have been asked!

Please note that professional photographers may appreciate it a bit less when you try to use their photos without licensing them correctly.

5. Include the photos in your emails. In your regularly email updates, show off the great photos that your guests are taking. People will certainly be interested to see them and it will remind them just how much they want to be with you.

# Embed Your Social On Your Site

Most Tour Operators do this, which is nice, but take care to pick the right social widgets. Frankly, most of them are crap.

Twitter especially offers little value. How many times have you seen a stream of Tweets on a website and then actually followed someone? Is it worth having this distraction on your site?

My favorite social media to embed is Instagram because the images look great on your site and actually help you sell your tours. The other widgets tend to be ugly and people's eyes will easily brush over them.

It's possible to embed Instagram on your home page and get a constant stream of new photos coming through, especially if you're following the previous tip of getting guests to tag you in. You can also do an embed on each of your tour listings and make sure photos only show up of that particular tour – all you need to do is create a specific hash-tag for each tour and you're off to the races.

Embedding Facebook albums is another possibility. This way, you can still keep uploading photos to Facebook without having to have the additional hassle of uploading photos to your website. What you can easily do is create a Facebook album for each tour, embed the album at the bottom of a tour, and go from there.

## Get People To Like Your Brand On Facebook - As Opposed To Liking Specific Pages On Your Site

Facebook offers lots of little widgets for you to embed on your site.

One is the ability to have a like button for a certain page of a site as opposed to the whole site. This means that they aren't liking your official page and you won't be able to stay in touch them via your Facebook status updates. This is a perfect example

This particular widget is a good idea on many blogs – it helps them make their blog posts go viral - but is a terrible idea for tour operators.

If people are going to like you, it's MUCH better that you're getting them to like your official page. There are many widgets which are easy to embed which offer this exact functionality. A word of advice, though: only do this if you have an actual, elaborated Facebook strategy as opposed to 'yeh we use Facebook'. Any action you ask people to take on your site needs to be all about getting people to take the steps towards a sale even if it's in the distant future.

## What Should You Post On Social? (Answer: Videos, Photos, Videos)

The key for all social media interaction is emotion. Always be thinking about how you are making people feel. Have you noticed that the posts that make people laugh, feel inspired, happy or angry are the ones that get the biggest reactions?

Photos are the main attraction on social media. They're also the easiest thing to upload and will help you stay in touch with past guests with much less hassle.

The best thing: it's SUPER easy. During a tour just snap photos and upload them. It takes one or two seconds to do and you're right there anyway. You can take 8 second videos on Instagram or Vine and have them synced to Facebook. Better yet, upload the videos directly to Facebook where you'll get much more engagement.

Take photos of people having fun but also be sure to upload great scenery shots or urban shots too. Make them wish they were there with you!

UPDATE - since the book was first released, data has come out showing that photos are now the worst thing to post on Facebook relative to how many people they show it to! (Maybe too many people were taking my advice.)

Facebook is at the moment engaged in massive war with Youtube to drive ascendancy with video. This means that in your case, the more video, the better.

In addition to this, here's a few more ideas for things to post up:

1. New testimonials. Posting testimonials on an occasional basis will remind people how awesome you are.
2. Awards or press. It's always exciting to see businesses that we like achieving success.
3. Upcoming special trips.
4. Articles about your area from other blogs or news sites. It's not just about keeping your business front of mind – you need to keep feeding the desire to come back to your part of the world. It's also a good way to maintain a relationship with fellow tourism businesses if you share their articles or the same with local bloggers.
5. Put links to your blog occasionally (if you have one).
6. Exclusive discounts.
7. Posts about your specialty. If you run a wine tour company, for example, you can share information and articles about wine. Easy!
8. Ask questions where people can share their own knowledge or preferences.
9. Play games. Post up photos and ask people to guess the spot.

Using Facebook or any other social media channel doesn't need to be complicated. There's no rocket science to it. Just post interesting stuff and do so regularly.

If you need inspiration, go and hit Like on 20 other businesses that are similar to yours from around the world.

*Sell More Tours*

They'll fill your feed every day with new ideas for your business to help you expand in all ways.

## Be That Fun Business On Facebook – Tips For Managing Social Successfully

Let's be real. When you use Facebook, I doubt you want to see your feed jammed with businesses trying to sell themselves. As a tour operator you have a cool advantage in that you can actually post interesting things up. Dental businesses don't have that kind of good fortune, so make the most of it!

I've talked about what TripAdvisor wants. Now, let's talk about what Facebook wants.

Facebook wants <u>active users.</u> Sound a bit like TripAdvisor? In fact, this is the main goal of all social media websites and the main metric that they are measured on in the news media.

When Facebook sees someone liking a post, their algorithm robot says "hey, let's show them more of that thing." Keep this in mind.

Some tips:

<u>1. Facebook is meant to be </u>fun. A place where you have fun and people can have fun with you. Make sure the photos you post up are either beautiful, quirky or funny. The whole goal of this exercise is to make people want to hang out with you.

<u>2. Keep a track of what causes interaction. </u>In your page statistics, you'll have access to see exactly how many

people have liked and seen a post. This is the gold right here – experiment with new types of posts and stop making the kinds of posts that people are ignoring.

The more engagement your users have with past posts, the more likely Facebook is to show your future posts. Focus on engagement.

3. Seek activity but in the right way. Knowing they need engagement, many business owners will often beg people for a comment and frame their posts in a needy, supplicating way. This is not the right way to do it: do everything to avoid coming across like this.

4. Don't post too much. One of the most common questions I get is 'how often should I post?' There's no answer to this question better than the statistics on your posts – likes, comments, views. Your fans will send the message to you louder and clearer (through their silence) than any guru! That being said, 3-4 times a week is a good rule IF you are posting up good stuff.

5. Give people a backstage pass to your business. The most valuable thing your business could ever create with someone is a personal connection. This is where someone knows who you are, what you do and likes you for it. Createthat connection by showing the hidden stuff in your business that other people might hide. For example, you could experience a vehicle breakdown, for example. People will empathize with you more than criticize and if you make light of it, you will be even more loved.

6. Respond to people's comments - don't just leave them hanging. When people comment they actually do respect a

response – in any case, I know I do! As with TripAdvisor, when you respond to people be personal and real. Show some personality! Shake off the 'cardboard PR persona' that has infected gigantic Fortune 500s and too many hapless tour operators.

7. Post outside of peak times. Facebook expert Jon Loomer conducted a case study using his own page to see what were the best times of day to post. Posts that went up late at night got much more reach and activity. This is when many people are still online but nearly all 'Official Pages' have shut up for the day! Loomer also found that when people began to log on in the morning, the posts were still right up there in the news-feed, waiting to be seen. The other pages he would normally have to compete with were too busy eating their breakfast to be posting on Facebook!

Less people are online at that time but because there's so much less competition in the Facebook feed you have almost exclusive access to them with your megaphone. You don't have to stay up late to do it necessarily, either. It's not too difficult to time your posts to go up when you're not around using available tools.

8. Ask simple, engaging questions. Short, snappy questions that require no thinking are the ones that will work the best. If there's one reason people are hanging around on Facebook, it's definitely not to make their brains work.

Example: "What's the 'hidden secret' restaurant in Chicago that you think EVERYBODY must know about and why? Leave a comment and share yours – and I'll share a couple of mine too." If you posted a question like that with a photo, you would definitely get engagement. Try it out and let me know how it goes (if it doesn't work for you, I will personally buy you a beer.)

Again, the purpose of nearly all good posting is not to sell directly but to just put yourself in people's minds. If someone is aware of you they're much more likely to use your service and recommend you. Build relationships! That's what Facebook is all about.

9. Avoid big gaps with no posting. For all social media, long disappearances make it look like your business is dead. It's better to delete links to your account than to have no posting at all.

10. Use call-to-actions from time to time. Call-to-actions (or CTAs) are when you ask for someone to take a particular action. This could mean asking them to tag themselves in a photo, leave a comment or click through to your website.

11. Get their emails. Last but very much not least, drive them to your email list any way you can. The average value per email subscriber is always multiples (generally many multiples) of a Facebook fan or Twitter follower. Which leads us to the next chapter.

# PART 3

# EMAIL MARKETING & MARKETING AUTOMATION

"It is easier to retain customers, than find new ones – and the best way to retain your customer base is to communicate to your customers regularly. Businesses can do this by using email marketing software programs." Paige Rowett, Tourismeschool.com

Imagine having a little slave robot that worked all day long doing marketing for your business without you having to do anything. How good would that be? You can entertain the little Roman Emperor inside of you without hurting anyone, ever. The great news for you keen marketers – and failed megalomaniacs – is that this kind of thing already exists. Your own little slave army exists and is ready to work for you. It's called marketing automation and stands out as THE most exciting new marketing tool that exists today.

Your email list is one of the most valuable assets considered by business brokers when judging the worth of a business. That's how important a good email list is – and when I say 'good', I mean 'active'.

The best thing about email marketing is that it's free, more or less. It's just a function of your time.

## Pick An Email Marketing Tool That Makes It Easy, Not A Hassle

Blogging. Social. SEO. TripAdvisor. Now email marketing? When will you have time to run your business?

Besides hiring someone, the next best bet is to use an easy tool.

The good news is that running a basic email marketing effort is not all that difficult. The extra-special-amazing news is that email marketing is possibly the HIGHEST ROI marketing activity that exists! In fact, data from research company Experian says that the average return on email marketing is 44.2x. (I'm not mathematician but that's a LOT of x!)

First things first, make sure you pick a tool rather than mass emailing people from your current email account using BCC. If you do this, there's a chance your email accounts (and those associated with your business) could be marked as spammers. You can trust my painful experience when I tell you that this is NOT a fun headache to deal with.

My favorite provider is Active Campaign which in my opinion wipes the floor with MailChimp, the brand that most operators use. Active Campaign is easier to use for me, has MUCH more powerful features and is built with marketing in mind. I love it. MailChimp is trying to play catch-up but the word has gotten out about Active Campaign. So much so, that most of my email marketing friends can't maintain a conversation for 5 minutes without mentioning it.

It's also cheap. At time of writing, you can use Active Campaign for free for a list of 2000 people if you accept their logo at the bottom of your emails. If not, you could just go with the $9 per month plan for 500 people. That being said, MailChimp tends to integrate much better with Wordpress so you have 6 of one and a half-dozen of the other.

More powerful tools for major heaving lifting are InfusionSoft, HubSpot and Ontraport. They offer more power than ActiveCampaign but will run you $250+ a month, can be ugly and also are difficult to use - without an expensive consultant to help you. I've never used these tools - I'm happy with ActiveCampaign - but if you're doing revenues of $250k+ you should check them out.

Some tour booking software providers will give you some capability for email marketing. It's nice to make use of this first, but specialist providers of email marketing software will do a better job for you if you're looking to step things up a notch. If you're just going to send the occasional 'hello' type of email, stick with whoever you've got.

Here's a few basic providers: ActiveCampaign, MailChimp, CampaignMonitor, ConstantContact, aWeber.

## Plain Emails Often Work Better Than Pretty Emails

Here's a fact that could surprise you: test after test (after test) shows that 'plain Jane' emails generally work better when compared to beautiful branded emails full of photos and fancy design. It may not be the case for you, but you should consider testing it.

The basic reason is simple: 'ad blindness'. As humans we've become so saturated by advertisements we tune out anything that LOOKS like an advertisement – and unfortunately, that will also include your nice email.

People tune out of communication that is generic and appears as 'one-to-many'. Compare this with plain text emails – your recipients KNOW that it's directed to many people, but the fact that these are written as if to one person means they're more likely to connect with it.

Plain doesn't mean there's no text formatting. The best plain emails are like a good blog post – there's SOME formatting (bold text, bullet points, the occasional image) but that's where they stop. You can even include a simple header that has your logo but that's where I'd leave it.

Another advantage to plain emails is that they work well on mobile devices, where 35-50% of your emails are now being opened.

A plain email can be prettied up a bit. You can create a simple header with your logo if you want but leave it there. You can use images if you want but just do it on a new line and make it take the full width of the email. Trying to wrap text around words in email only leads to headaches.

## Scared Of Being An Annoying Spammer? Don't Be

OK, so we all hate spam. Put that in the 'shocking news' section of tomorrow's news, please.

But I have good news for you: emailing people who themselves chose to hear from you is NEVER spam (there's just one exception: when they ask you to stop, and then you need to make sure they're off your list or you could get into hot water.) There's a definition for the word spam and part of it includes 'unsolicited'.

Email can be and often IS annoying, yet if you have a small business people will often enjoy hearing from you, especially if the email feels personal. How often do you get emails from small businesses? Almost never, right?

People enjoy hearing from local businesses simply because it's so rare. Most email campaigns come from gigantic travel websites (at least in my case!) and this can get annoying, such that when you get an email from a local business it's actually a nice surprise.

Because you're not an unknown entity and you have a small business, your email is nearly always welcome... so long as you're not sending 5 emails a day, because that could begin to become a little irritating. Just saying.

# HOW TO GET THE MOST OUT OF YOUR EMAIL LIST

"What should I send in my emails?" Ahh, the universal question. If you're like most people who haven't yet tried email campaigns, you may be scared of annoying people with spam.

Before we get on to that, there's three types of people who would on your list: hot prospects, long-term prospects and past guests.

Let's deal with long-term prospects and past at this moment (we'll get onto how to deal with hot prospects a bit later in the book.) These people can go onto the same general email list. The good news is that for your service to stay in people's minds, you don't need to email all that often. You'll see blog posts telling you to email once a week or more but that doesn't apply in this particular case, rather to hot prospects.

Here are some tips:

1. Don't make ALL of your emails naked attempts to sell trips. Find other topics to talk about so they don't feel like you're non-stop pumping them for cash. I doubt I'm the only person who hates being repetitively slammed with requests for money. The only exception to this is if your tour business is runs special event type tours which you put on now and then.

2. Send behind the scenes emails. For some reason, people REALLY dig behind the scenes info. I have a buddy with

a business where they share ALL of their revenue details – to the exact cent – on their blog every single month. Each month this is by far the most popular blog post they write and the funny thing is that it's all about them.

3. Keep appetites whetted about upcoming events and test out new ideas. This is the best thing about having an email list - you can use it to fill in the down months and test out ideas for new tour types.

4. Send out tips related to your tour type and area. If you run food tours you can share tips for amazing, unknown restaurants. Winery tours can share advice and insider tips about wine. If you run more generic city tours, that's fine too: just share tips about the city you run tours in.

5. Send out photos. Why not? If we've learned one thing about photos, it is that people can't get enough of them.

6. For the love of everything good, don't call it a newsletter. I kind of enjoy newsletters from small business (I'm a little wacky) but the stats are in - they show that people are less likely to click on something with a name like Newsletter or eNews. The primary reason for this is that newsletters feel like a drag. They're a drag for you to make which nearly always comes through in the writing process, making them a drag to read. While it's always good to have some kind of marketing schedule behind the scenes, you don't need to broadcast this to the world.

7. Keep yourself front of mind. How frequently should you send the emails? At least once a month and no less. Depending on the kind of tours you run, you may want to send more. If you run lots of special events, it's more

appropriate to send more emails.

8. <u>That being said, only email when you have something to say</u>. This comes back to the forced feeling of email newsletters, which tend to bore people over time because the person who is doing it is bored themselves.

9. <u>Creative descriptive subjects for your emails</u>. The subject is the most important thing and will determine how many people open the email you send. 'October Newsletter' or 'Update' can be improved upon. You should work hard on your subject line trying to come up with the best one possible.

10. <u>Make sure the opening lines are grabbing</u>. The first two sentences of an email are what your reader will see as a preview in their email inbox. This is known as a 'preheader' or 'teaser'. You need to focus on making sure that those few words do the job of getting people interested in opening the email and hearing what you have to say.

11. <u>Test and track</u>. By sending a variety of emails and and tracking them, you'll build a picture over time as to which emails people find interesting and which are duds.

12. <u>Send in your own name, not the company's</u>. I've said it before and I'll continue saying it until your ears bleed: business needs to be personal. The money-printing competitive advantage you have over gigantic-mega-huge-corporations is that you're NOT a gigantic-mega-huge-corporation!

Part of that is sending email in your own name, not your company's. Just mention the company name in the subject or in brackets so that the recipient knows where the email is coming from. You can do something like this: Mark Bickley (GeoTrips).

While writing this chapter, I received an email from a small business owner named Christine. She wanted to thank all her guests for making the previous year so wonderful for her. She included a couple of pictures of kangaroos hanging out near her property and signed off.

You know how I felt after reading this email? I felt great. I really felt happy for Christine! The strangest thing is her email didn't even try to sell or be entertaining. It was just a personal thank-you. Now Christine's business is at the front of my mind.

Even if an email isn't one-to-one, it still does feel personal to receive an email directly from the owner. Go ahead, give it a try.

13. Don't be overly creative (read: deceptive) in your subject lines. This annoys your readers and can lose sales. While it helps to write creative subject lines for your emails, promising one thing and delivering another is not going to help. In the emails I send out, I try to be as literal as possible, no games.

14. Make sure your unsubscribe button is nowhere near any other links in your email, including the links in your signature. This is important because on mobile devices when you're using your thumbs, it's hard sometimes to click on the right link.

## AUTORESPONDERS: WIN THOSE DOUBTERS OVER

Autoresponders are the soldiers of that little slave army you can have that I mentioned earlier in this book. Autoresponders are NOT the automatic responses you receive from people saying "Hello. We wish to thank you for your correspondence. It has been received and we will endeavor to reply within 24 hours"

Instead, it's like a marketing assistant that works 24-7 to increase your sales, just without the dungeon, the whip and the starvation. The great thing is you just need to set it up once and it just runs and runs and runs.

Autoresponders are just a series of emails that are automatically sent to a recipient over a defined period (hence the 'auto' in 'autoresponder.') An example campaign would send out 5 emails over 10 days, and then continue to send more over time but with less frequency. For example, you could be sending out a bunch of tips for people arriving to your city – a new tip every few days.

The purpose of autoresponders is to convert hot leads into actual sales. But how do we get someone to actually sign up to our list? They need a good reason! That good reason is nearly always a free guide of some kind, leading to the next tip in this book.

To see an autoresponder in action visit tourismtiger.com/videos/ and sign up. You'll receive a series of emails as part of our own email campaign efforts.

# Juice Up Your AutoResponder: Offer A Free Guide They Can Get Via Email

Ever heard the expression "you need to make 7 touches to get the sale?"

People won't remember you just from the one visit to your site. Some will, but what if we can get the rest to join your tour, too?

If you have their email, you can stay in touch with them and provide them information... automatically. Build a relationship with them – no extra work required!

For example, a visitor to your website might sign up for your "10 Hidden Secrets of Lisbon That Nearly ALL Visitors Miss Out On" free ebook.

They'll get the ebook and then over the next month or two, receive simple emails with tips on how to enjoy their time in Lisbon more from your autoresponder software. Email after email keeps your business front of mind and you don't have to do anything to keep it running.

It's a proven way to increase sales and the joy of it is that once you set things up, it's completely hands-off. Don't want to write an ebook? Make the offer a '7 Email Guide To Lisbon's Unknown Corners' and then all you have to do is write the 7 emails... and boom, done! It may be the most valuable thing you ever do in your business.

# GETTING PEOPLE ONTO YOUR LIST

Pop-ups are the best way to get people on to your list if you're happy to annoy your visitors a little. Pop-ups, like advertising, are a funny thing. Everyone says they hate them but they still kick butt! The reality is that people hate them far less than they say they do, and you'll turn off far fewer people than you think you might.

(What are pop-ups? Pop-ups are the little forms that jump into your face when you visit a website, inviting you to put your email in to subscribe to their list.)

The key to making pop-ups valuable is to offer something that's valuable, such as the free ebook guide of your city that I mentioned earlier in the book. If don't offer anything in exchange ("subscribe to my newsletter!" pop-ups always suck) then yes: people will get annoyed with you.

If you don't want to use pop-ups – and heck, I see why – there are many options, such as a prominent opt-in area at the top of your website or in the sidebar. Another type of pop-up growing in popularity right now is one that slides up from the bottom right after the visitor has scrolled a certain percentage of a page. This is less annoying to visitors.

## Marketing Automation: Sending The Right Emails To People At The Right Time

Imagine you have a new, special tour coming up. You want to send a bunch of emails about it because you know a lot of people are interested in it, but you also know that it's irrelevant to about 50% of your list and you don't want to annoy them. What do you do?

The answer to this is marketing automation.

Let's just say you run a mountain bike tour company and you're launching a new 2 week trip to South Africa. You send out a couple of emails about it letting people know it's happening. 35% of people open at least one of the emails and the other 65% ignore them both. Wouldn't it be better to stop sending the emails about this special trip to that 65% in order so that they don't unsubscribe – and you keep the chance to continue emailing them later?

From there, you continue sending emails about the South Africa trip to the people who are interested in that trip and then leave the other people alone. The best thing? It's possible to do this automatically.

It's possible to take it even FURTHER (yeh buddy, this is when the good sauce happens!) If someone on your email list visits your website and goes to the section about, say, custom group wine trips, it's possible to move them into a small autoresponder series of 2 emails you have prepared about custom group wine trips. You might email that person a recent testimonial you've received for your custom group wine trips, a brochure or a few photos. This is striking while the iron is hot – sending an email to someone at the exact time that they're ready.

With automation, you only email people about topics they have interest in. They show their interest by opening an email, clicking on a link in an email or by visiting a part of your site.

It doesn't take a genius to see the potential impact on your sales. For too long, companies have been sending out generic catch-all emails because of their inability to segment their list into various components based on people's behavior, location or interest. This is no longer a problem.

It is like magic and has taken the entire online marketing world by storm. Start-ups like HubSpot, InfusionSoft, GetVero, Ontraport and Marketo offer this kind of software. MailChimp has just started to offer it but as before, I'm not a fan of the Chimp and would recommend something else for this. Active Campaign is the software I'm personally using for this kind of thing.

Marketing automation is a tough subject to summarize into a small section in one book (I have 4 books on my Kindle just about this topic). It's also something that can be quite complex to set up if that wasn't already obvious. In most cases it'd be best to use the help of a professional to set it up and make sure you get started on the right track. There's no lack of them, either: nearly all the software providers above have certified consultants who can help you on your journey. While the process is complicated and can be expensive depending on your budget, remember that there is a good reason it's exploding despite all this: it works.

# Turning Subscribers Into Sales

Selling to your email list is the final goal of this. Customers are why we have email software, email lists, and email newsletters.

But, how do we turn people from passive email subscribers into paying visitors without pushing them too hard and turning them off? For Tour Operators, it's not too hard. You have a product that people are interested in and that product costs money. People will be fine to be sold to from time to time if they like you.

Some thoughts:

1. Use the PS area. The PS area is one of the most viewed of all emails and even if you send an email that's not trying to sell something you can use the 'PS' area to encourage a specific action. It's one of the most read parts of emails besides the first line! Example: "PS. We just opened up bookings for our next trip to America. They're filling up fast! Don't miss out. Info here: example.com/america"

When people the PS it can generate a spark of curiosity and for whatever reason, it feels like it's more personalized even though this is not the case. I've known about this trick for nearly 10 years now and it still works on me to do this day.

2. Basically no one buys after just one email. You need to warm people up and build that relationship gradually. It's not a case of sending one email guide and watch the cash

pour on.

3. Avoid being the annoying salesperson who uses insistent language such as BOOK NOW!!!! or CLICK HERE!!! Do people actually think that if you use four exclamation marks instead of two, that they'll get more sales? Seeing laziness like this really yanks my chain.

4. Make the emails look great on mobile devices. If they don't, you're missing out because over 50% of emails are now opened on mobile devices, a figure that climbs every single month.

5. Track your conversions. How do you know if email is working for you if you're not tracking it? Just like with any other marketing channel, it's necessary to know how many sales and booking inquiries are coming from your list subscribers. I'll get into tracking conversions later in this book but I can also refer you to Analytics experts who can set this kind of thing up for you.

6. Nearly all emails need to include a Call to Action. If you're selling a new tour in your email then the CTA is obvious - "Book Your Spot Now" - but what if you're sending something else? No fear – just try to get them to like your Facebook page or follow you on Twitter. Even better, use the PS of your email (as mentioned before) to nudge them into an impulse booking of a trip.

# PART 4

# A BASIC GUIDE TO OPTIMIZING YOUR SITE FOR GOOGLE

Search Engine Optimization (SEO) is the practice of modifying your website's presence to make it appear relevant to things people are searching for on Google. The goal of doing this is to appear higher in the search results for various terms – or keywords, as they're generally called.

Google will look at your website and what the internet is saying about you (or not saying) to determine your ranking.

SEO has changed a lot in the last 10 years. Simple tactics which used to reliably drive you to number one now can see you penalized and disappeared from the rankings.

Google has really progressed as a search engine and is much better at understanding the actual intent of what someone is searching for. This means that a lot of the tips and tricks of yesteryear have become outdated.

# Google: A Brief Explanation

Google started at a time when search engines generated horrendously mediocre results - you could search for term after term after term and not find anything remotely related to what you were looking for.

Ridiculously, these other search engines were doing this deliberately to get people to spend more time searching – and as a result, more time looking at ads. Seriously - one company passed on the opportunity to buy Google's technology in its early days because it delivered people to their destination too quickly!

The underlying root problem behind these terrible results was that search engines were unable to understand what websites were actually about . Teaching machines to understand text is extremely tough.

In the midst of this environment, the founders of Google made two key discoveries which enabled them to build an amazing search engine. Both discoveries remain highly relevant to their business today.

Discovery 1: More Links = More Credibility. The more links point to a website from other quality websites, the more reliable and trustworthy that website is. Because of this discovery, they built a gigantic map of the web, showing how all the different websites were linking to each other. Websites that were receiving the most links (especially from other websites which also had a lot of links pointing towards them) received higher priority in the search results.

Discovery 2: Anchor Text = Relevance. The words used in

a link, otherwise known as anchor text, were an accurate representation of the topic of that page. When you click on a link, the anchor text is the words that you click on. For example, if a link looks like this: White House, the anchor text in this case would be "White House", and Google then knows that the particular website receiving the link is relevant to the term "White House."

These two discoveries in combination meant that Google could grow at an explosive rate. The issue that surfaced, however, was that as Google grew in importance, websites began to engage in deliberate attempts to manipulate their algorithm to receive more traffic. We started to see websites attempting to rank artificially by trying to get links to their websites using shady or spammy means.

As a result, a huge proportion of Google's work since that point has been trying to come up with algorithmic methods to stamp out spammers and ensure that quality floats to the top.

One of Google's driving financial incentives is to deliver spam-free, quality results. I've talked about this before in the book – the more you align yourself with the financial incentives of the companies that deliver visitors to your website, the more you set yourself up for long-term gains.

Whenever you work on your website or pay for someone to do it, avoid appearing spammy (or overly spammy). If you're doing something JUST because it might deliver you a link and wouldn't realistically bring you any other benefits – such as receiving actual visitors from that link – my advice would just be this: tread carefully.

# HOW GOOGLE UNDERSTANDS A WEBSITE

One of Google's most important and ongoing missions is to understand websites just how humans understand them. They're nowhere near this point at the moment but they're getting good at a surprising rate.

In the early days, Google used crude systems to read a website. You could take a keyword such as "New York Walking Tours" and repeat it over again on your website and get a high ranking. Practices like this forced Google to engage in a continuous cat-and-mouse game with website owners as they dealt with ever increasing levels of trickery that people used on their site.

You may have noticed that by and large, these issues have faded to the background. It's rare to see a website rank in Google if uses simple, spammy tactics like seen from 2002 to 2008.

In the effort to combat spammy websites, Google is forced to use machines to determine the relevance of keywords and have created many high-powered algorithms to that end. Google doesn't really publish the information about how they determine the relevancy of a website, but they do reveal information in patents. Here's an example:

"A computer-implemented method and apparatus defines a keyword class vector. A set of seed keywords is determined from a set of keywords and first and second most similar keywords from the set of seed keywords are then determined. A class vector is determined from first and second keyword vectors associated with the first and second most similar keywords. "

Clear as mud, right? I'll do my best to explain it.

Google now understands a site by looking at how the words interact with each other. For example, 'White House' could mean a residence for a powerful person in America OR it could just be a beautiful white house. How can Google tell which is which? By looking at the words surrounding the term 'White House' – such as Washington, president, Democrats, Republicans - Google is able to determine the relevance of that page. If it's about a nice white house, there will be housing related terms instead such as 'fence', 'flowers' or 'a graceful home'. This means that instead of just using a keyword over and over, your page needs to use a lot of rich language to describe a certain concept. This is how Google knows your page is relevant.

## USER EXPERIENCE MATTERS TO GOOGLE – AND IS GROWING EVER MORE IMPORTANT

Nowadays, when Google announces a change to their algorithm it generally will have something to do with user experience.

For example, here's a few things they've announced that you can do to help your site.

1. Make sure your website loads fast (2010).
2. Ensure a good experience on mobile devices (2013).
3. Not the top of a site with ads (2012).
4. High quality, original content (2011).

Independent testing has shown that websites with a high bounce rate have lower rankings, although it could be correlation instead of causation. Later in this book, we'll cover the topic of how to reduce your bounce rate and keep more visitors around, because keeping more visitors for longer is a good thing.

The basic conclusion from this is that while Google does continually obfuscate, you should take their advice and give your users the BEST experience possible. This feels almost as obvious as telling you not to put your hand in a raging fire, but I've NEVER visited a tour operator website that has been built correctly according to Google's standards and as you can imagine, I've visited many. That's right - quite literally 0% of tour operator websites are built correctly and this book is part of my mission to change that.

## Piggy-Back On The Work Of Your Competition

I could easily write a book just on the topic of search engine optimization. It's an in-depth, complicated topic but here's the good news: if you nail the basics, 80% of your work is done.

The even better news is that it's impossible for your competitors to hide any SEO work that they do. It's open in the air for you to see, because if Google can see it, so you can you. You can make VERY good use of that by tracking the tactics and strategies of similar businesses and adopting them for your own.

The #1 hack to cost-effective marketing with Google, paid traffic or free, is to piggy-back on the work of other operators like this.

Chances are you have a bunch of competitors out there. Many of them have done SEO. ALL of them have left a bread-crumb trail.

How many tour operators in the world have a similar business to you? Some of those businesses are kicking BUTT. Why not check out their activity? Why not call them up and ask them for tips? What's stopping you?

# Stay Away From The Big Dogs

Before you fight, you need to know your weight before you step into the boxing ring. If you're a small company in a big market, you may struggle to compete on the highest volume search terms.

The cardinal sin here is to go for the tourism terms in your city or area that gets the most searches each month.

Why is this such a bad idea?

Two reasons.

<u>Disproportionate competition</u> - People will largely compete for the biggest piece of gold and leave the rest sitting off to the side. Even worse, you have to deal with the likes of TripAdvisor and Viator going after the same piece of pie.

<u>The more generic a keyword, the less people are likely to buy</u> - When someone searches for a non-specific keyword such as "New York Tours" they are less likely to convert into a sale and are probably just starting their research. "New York Walking Tours" will perform a bit better. "New York Pizza Tours" would convert fantastically. When the visitor has a very specific idea of what they want, and you meet that specific idea, it's a match made in SEO heaven. The key thing to remember here is that rankings mean nothing if they don't generate sales, so you need to always focus on relevance instead of volume.

Unless you're a very big dog in your market you should be thinking a bit more laterally.

Tourism operators beat their heads against the wall trying

to compete for the top traffic terms with people who have budgets quite literally ten times the size of theirs. If you hustle a lot it COULD happen for you but it's a much smarter idea to go after other keywords.

That's when we look for keyword ideas that we CAN compete on.

The first step is to brainstorm as many related terms and synonyms related to your business as possible. From there, we investigate those terms and then explore new ones using online tools.

## Keyword Ideas: Get Ideas From Some Great Tools

Besides using your imagination to determine what you want to rank for in Google, there's a bunch of tools out there which will help you brainstorm ideas.

Two basic free tools in everyone's arsenal are Google Adwords Keyword Planner and Ubersuggest, but KeywordTool.io is now my favorite. Keyword Planner gives you hard data on how many people are searching for each terms, but is terrible for brainstorming because it often gives a very narrow range of selections for you to look at. KeywordTool.io on the other hand is a great way to brainstorm, so what I often do is just hammer it looking for suggestions and then transfer the results over to Google Keyword Planner to check how much traffic each of my ideas gets.

Both tools are highly limited in their scope and should not be seen as the be-all end-all, so for other free tools, consider KeywordDiscovery.com and Soovle.com.

Use paid tools if you're deadly serious about dedicating a bunch of energy to succeeding in this space. My favorite SEO tool in the world is also brand new - it's called SEMcompass.com. Being involved in the industry I've been lucky enough to get an insider's sneak peek before launch and let me tell you that this thing is legit.

It rolls the capability of the world's best SEO tools together into one (cheaper) tool, so rather than paying for four separate memberships, you can just sign up for this one.

*Sell More Tours*

For other paid tools, checkout SEMrush, Raven Tools, Moz.com, KeywordSpy and Wordtracker.

## Keyword Ideas: Piggy-Back On The Work Of Related Companies

Golly, I love this topic.

Similar operators just like you, all around the world, have spent thousands of dollars on SEO and all of it is lying bare for any observer to make the most of it.

When most people start on this, they tend to make the mistake of just copying their competitors flat out while ignoring all other methods. This is not clever. It's worth looking at your competition but don't stop there.

Besides visiting your competitor websites, check out those of similar operators around the world. Go through them with a fine tooth comb. Don't just look at the title or headline. Are they using synonyms on their page you wouldn't have thought to have used? Are they being more descriptive of their tours than you?

By looking at similar operators in other cities and other countries, you'll find some surprises. For example, did you know that in England, they use the term car hire and in the USA, they use the term car rental?

The next step is to find the various keywords your competitors are ranking for. I love doing this because the results always have a couple of nice surprises.

The best tool for finding treasure troves of undiscovered keywords being used by other sites to rank in Google is

SEMrush.com, but you can now access the capability of SEMrush in SEMcompass.com. This would be my recommended step.

## Keyword Ideas: Get Clever with Alternate Keywords

If you follow the earlier ideas in this section, you'll no doubt arrive at some surprising keyword ideas

Let's dig deeper, though. Let's get lateral. If we include many terms that only get searched for every now and then, this will eventually add up to our big success.

What are other terms do people use to describe the kind of tours you offer?

You might call it a walking tour. What are some other terms?

- Guided tour
- Escorted tour
- By foot (I just discovered this term in SEMcompass. I would never have thought to use the words 'by foot').
- Tour guides (people looking for the person offering the tour as opposed to the product).
- Day tour
- Sightseeing tour (this is semi-relevant.. people searching for this would be looking for bus tours, primarily.)

You might call it New York. How else do people call New York?

- New York City
- Nyc

- Manhattan
- Manhattan New York
- Lower Manhattan
- Downtown NYC

Think about other geographic terms. People do include the names of states and provinces in their searches (such as "Tours Miami Florida" "Tours Miami FL"), something forgotten about by most tour operators.

Searchers will often mention a specific sight or location. For example, 20 people every month search for "Times Square Walking Tour".

Let's be realistic: in certain markets, you can be as lateral as you want but if you have 250+ tour operators in your city and you have a tour that isn't unique in some way, you may struggle. The first step in that case is to work on your product.

## What To Do With These Keywords: Give Your Site A Great Title And Headlines For Both Google AND Humans

If you Google something, the title of each link in the results is usually the title element of the website. It's Google's biggest indicator as to what your site is about, which makes it crucially important to your rankings.

Your title can only have a few words in it, so it shows what your business really is about. The same applies to the few headlines you have on your site. It's your big way to tell Google what you're about.

Some basic tips:

<u>1. Don't use the same keyword twice in a title or headline</u>. I've seen sites knocked down 10 pegs just for this reason. For example: 'New York Tours | New York Walking Tours' is not good – it's unnatural and spammy.

<u>2. Write for humans</u>. 'John's Tours | Philadelphia Walking Tours | Historical Tours Pennsylvania | Guided Walks' is written for robots.

<u>3. Make use of your keyword research to create longer keywords</u>. For example, 'Walking Tours Boston' could easily turn into 'Guided Walking Tours Boston' or 'Historical Walking Tours Boston'. You've kept your main keyword there but with little bit of potential bonus on top

of that.

Don't forget that ACTUAL HUMANS read this stuff when they search Google and based on what they see in the title and the Meta Description, they will decide what to click.

## What To Do With These Keywords: Write Some Great Tour Descriptions

Oh, how the angels weep and the demons gnash their teeth when they see a tour description with no detail.

Put aside the SEO for a second. Having a great tour description will help your sales if you can give people a detailed idea as to exactly what will happen on your tours.

The added benefit is that helps you get more traffic from Google, too, because you'll start showing up in many more Google searches.

Lots of information doesn't have to be ugly if you include lots of sub-headlines. Go for 1000+ words if you can and use many of those different keywords that you discovered. You'll find the rewards in small increments of traffic will add up across all the different pages of your site and end up having a genuine impact on your bottom line.

You may think 1000+ words is difficult, but think about the sort of information people need: basic details, full itinerary, a bit of information about the places being visited, FAQs, what the guest needs to bring, pickup points.... It becomes tough to keep it below 1000 words!

## What To Do With These Keywords: Optimize Your Images And Links

Now you have a great, long tour description what's the perfect accompaniment?

Images! If you're going to upload images, it's worth uploading them to Google.

Three tips:

1. Make sure the file name reflects the image. File names such as DC_1022.JPG are fairly useless to Google. How are they meant to look at your image and know what it's about? At some point in the future they might be able to do this, but not right now.

2. Use different terms for the names of each image. You see it all the time where someone names their images New-York-Walking-Tour1.JPG and then New-York-Walking-Tour2.JPG. Mix it up a little bit.

3. Add an alt tag. If you use Wordpress or any other major software, use it to add an alt tag, which is a written description of what an image is. This gives search engines a nice little hint as to what your photo is about.

Optimizing images is generally not going to have a big impact but if you're going to upload images, you might as well make the most of it. Tourism especially is a highly visual field compared to most other business niches, so with correct optimization you have a decent chance at getting some visitors from Google Images.

Also use the keywords to optimize your internal links – those links between various pages in your site.

# CREATE PAGES FOR SUB-NICHES & SPECIAL EVENTS

Did you know there's a winery tour operator in the United States that specializes in taking gay and lesbian groups on tours?

I would never have thought of catering to that niche, but someone did.

The world is full of sub-niches – stamp collectors, model train builders, gothic music lovers, Italian ice cream connoisseurs, bird lovers, school groups, religious groups and sporting groups.

How can you cater to these people?

Taking the winery tour example, you can create a 'winery and brewery' option for those groups who may be taking people who don't like wine. A reluctant husband, for example.

You could create a specific page for school groups, as teachers are often looking for field day ideas. The list goes on. Be creative! While it's doubtful that creating a page for teachers looking to do day trips will explode your business overnight, there's a chance! Even if creating 10 new pages for various sub-niches only increases your business by 5 percent, it's very much worth the time and effort.

<u>Think About the Special Events That People Celebrate In Their Lives</u>

There's no physical limit to the amount of pages you can

have on your site, so why not create some special ones for people who are celebrating personal events?

When people search for ideas for special events you have a chance at showing up in the results.

It will take you an afternoon to brainstorm a few different products out and list them on your site. You'll most likely generate just the occasional booking from them but who knows – you could find yourself on the top of Google for 'bachelor party ideas Johnsonville' and have a continuous stream of drunken guests to enjoy yourself with (hooray!)

The tour and activity business aligns perfectly with this kind of niche and you don't even need to clutter up your home page. What many companies do is have a 'Special Events' or 'Special Tours' page where they list out all the different types of special occasions that can be catered for.

## Meta This And Meta That – What Works And What Doesn't?

There's a mind-boggling amount of contradictory SEO advice out there on the internet. SEO changes rapidly and as such, you may read an article that's out of date without realizing it. Many times, a freshly written article will be out of date before it's even published because the author's knowledge isn't current. This happens in the case of part-timers who don't follow the industry closely and will often give incorrect advice without realizing it's obsolete. Unfortunately, this is something very common in the tourism industry – not long before writing this chapter I watched a video containing SEO advice for hotel owners which was five years behind the times.

Here's a 2 minute rundown:

A website is built using code which lays out the appearance of all the images and text on your site.

In that code there are also sections which communicate directly with Google. For example, when you run a search have you ever wondered where they get the neat little descriptions of websites that are sitting there? You can actually tell Google what description you want it to use.

Here's the basic tags and elements that you need to know about:

Meta Title - the meta title of your site is without a doubt the most important part of your website when it comes to

SEO. As mentioned before, this is the title of your site that will show up when people Google for you. Keep it super relevant and make sure it contains the most important keyword you are trying to rank for.

Meta Description - as the name implies, this is the small description of your site that you give to Google. It doesn't have a direct impact on your rankings but it is important because a good meta description affects how many people click on the link to go through to your website. Your rankings then improve because more searchers are interested in your page than the pages listed above yours.

You may have noticed that Google bolds the text that you have searched for in the results. As a result, do include some super relevant keywords in your description but be sure to maintain the focus of the meta description on being readable and attracting people to your site. Make sure to have a unique meta description written for each page.

Meta Keywords - meta keywords are a relic of the past and for many years have had no impact whatsoever on rankings. It's also a basic test as to whether someone is worth listening to about SEO – if they tell you to use meta keywords, run the other way.

H1, H2, H3 - These are headlines which help Google determine which is the most important text on the page. They used to be enormously important; they are now just very important. The H1 headline on your website is the primary headline on the page – so you can imagine why Google lends this some importance.

Alt Tags - If you have ever hovered over an image and seen

a bit of text which explains the text, that is called an alt tag. The general conventional wisdom is that you should be doing this, but I must admit I've never seen an instance where a website updated its alt tags and suddenly shot up in the rankings. Despite this, it's still best practice so you should do it. Alt tags can be used on pretty much everything but are most commonly used in images and links.

<u>Bold & Italics -</u> Like alt tags, if it works – which is a big if - it plays a very small factor. I always recommend that people use bold and italics not for SEO, but for readability. When someone is bolding all the keywords on a page that they want to rank for, it's really quite irritating and gets my goat! Use bold text as it was designed to be used – to call attention to important things.

# SHOULD I BLOG OR SHOULD I NOT?

It's all too easy to say 'YES! BLOG!" This is the sort of advice you'll find repeatedly around the internet.

Blogging does not work out for many people who try it. The principle reason is that they're not passionate about it, they don't dedicate time to it and most importantly, they don't have a good plan in place. They just write about whatever comes into their head. Without a plan, you're destined to fail.

If you're blogging just because you read it in a book and it seems like a nice idea, don't even start. Blogging is all-or-nothing - decide whether to dive all the way in or just leave it alone.

Don't get me wrong. I do recommend blogging as a practice and it will work out wonderfully for you if you do it with energy, planning and persistence. Just make sure that once you've started that you never stop.

Remove the dates from your blog posts and focus on making your blog a useful resource. This gives a timeless nature to the content and removes the pressure from you of having to update your blog all the time.

Blog With a Bigger Goal

Imagine that you were to have an awesome blog with loads of tips about your area. Could you convert it into a book of some sort? I'm not talking a Lonely Planet-esque guide. Many ebooks nowadays have 20-50 pages in them.

If you begin your blogging journey with this higher level strategy in mind, you could well end up with a decent body of work which could be turned into a handy resource. This will help you with sales, too – who wouldn't want to go on a tour with the guide of "Walking New York"? Many guests would pay a premium for the privilege!

# Blogging And Informational Resources: What To Write About

Most people will turn to some sort of keyword research to decide what to blog about. Following the previous chapters you may find some ideas but I want to deal with a misconception about blogging.

Blog posts rarely lead to a sale on the first visit, so you shouldn't be blogging all day long about your tours. The best blogs are valuable information resources. Then, when someone wants to book a tour, you're on the front of their mind. Even better if they have subscribed to your 7 email autoresponder with tips for the best things to do in Adelaide.

Let's get a bit lateral, then. The TripAdvisor forums are GREAT place to get blogging ideas (Travllr is another). This is where people go to ask questions about their upcoming trips – and where you can find insight into the kinds of things that people are searching for in Google.

On the Paris TripAdvisor forum, here's some recent forum topics:

What would you do in Paris for 2 days only?

Hotels around 1-6 districts

Getting around metro?

Places to eat near Moulin Rouge

Buying Louvre Tickets online

What to do in Paris with children?

There's lots of good ideas right there for blog posts and informational resources – all you need to do is cherry pick them.

Either way, insert a mention automatically at the top and bottom of the blog post pointing to your tours, if you have nothing else to point them at. As someone reads your blog post, they'll be pointed towards your more valuable content or your email sign up form. There's Wordpress plugins that allow you to do that and it's also a capability we have activated for our own customers.

Beyond this, the internet is swamped with 'blog post ideas'. Every single self-styled blogging guru has at least one post with '101 Blog Topic Ideas' or some-such. A quick Google search will unearth a mountain of information.

Later on in this book, I'll look at how to take a blog post visitor and turn them into a paying customer.

## GET RID OF DEAD PAGES

Over time, a website grows a bit old and hairy. There's many times when you'll create a page for a specific event and then just leave it there orphaned, or you may stop offering a particular tour.

When pages are removed or moved, there's still a chance that there's a link to those pages somewhere else in the website – for example, a previous blog post. You could be linking out to other websites that are now dead.

This isn't just an annoyance for users - it's also something that could well hurt you in Google.

It's important to make sure you do a regular check – say, every 3-6 months – to look for issues. The mental trap here is to assume that your website has no issues. Of course you'd assume that – the whole point of this exercise is to check for things you have forgotten and how do you know if you have forgotten it or not?

Add your website to Google Webmaster Tools if you have not done so already and do a basic run-through of the different areas of information that is provided there.

Additional tools worth checking out are Screaming Frog, Xenu Link Sleuth and the simply-named Brokenlinkcheck.com.

## WITH SEO, IT PAYS TO KEEP THE FUTURE IN MIND

As you attempt to gain the trust of Google and increase your ranking, it's probable that you'll find people offering shady (or semi-shady) advice about ways for you to do so.

The SEO world is split between cautious professionals and cowboys. There are no regulations in this field so the cowboys in the field may help you to a temporary bump in rankings and traffic but in the end leave you highly vulnerable to an algorithm change from Google – or even worse, a penalty.

Part of the fault for this sits on the shoulders of small business owners who place undue pressure on SEO consultants to get results NOW. The fact of the matter is that the best SEO campaigns move slowly – in many cases you may wonder if anything is happening! Yet, you will see a steady, continuous, upwards trend.

I'll give you an example. I mentioned earlier in this book that one of Google's key discoveries was that anchor text used in links (as a reminder, anchor text is the word or words that you click on in a link, such as '[click here](#)' or '[Sydney Tours](#)') was a great way to measure relevance for a site. This meant that a New York tour operator who had 20 links with the anchor text 'New York tours' would rank highly for the term New York tours.

You can imagine what happened next. People went BONKERS building links all over the place pointing back to their website with the anchor text of the exact term they wanted to rank for! Before long, many small businesses had 100, 200 or even 1000 links back to their website using the exact same anchor text.

Blind Freddy could have told you that Google was going to crack down on this, but with the short-term thinking prevalent in corners of the SEO industry, no heed was paid to this - until Penguin, a cute name for an infamous Google update which crunched thousands of small businesses worldwide.

Google wasn't particularly happy with such blatant manipulation of their algorithm, so what they did was simple and effective: any website where more than ~60% of the links pointing to it used the same anchor text was penalized. Overnight, hundreds of thousands of websites disappeared from the top 10 of Google, many of them small businesses just like yours or mine.

Untold numbers of people lost their businesses and in some cases, everything - we're talking divorces, bankruptcies and foreclosures. All because they depended on a cheap, short-term trick to attempt to rise to the top of Google. If you depend on a website to maintain business income, don't mess with it. Always align your practices with Google's own financial incentives and you will mostly come out on top. It just takes time.

This is why you shouldn't hire SEO agencies that have 'secret sauce' methods. Evaluate all practices with an eye to the future – is this something that Google will realistically crack down later on? If your agency doesn't tell you what you're doing, how can you monitor this?

# DID YOU KNOW?

## I WILL SEND FREE UPDATES TO THIS BOOK

More tips and tricks will be added to later editions of this book. I'll email you the new chapters for free as they are added! Visit tourismtiger.com/bookupdates/

I'll also be releasing FREE video tutorials about how to implement many of the techniques described in this book at the same URL: tourismtiger.com/bookupdates/

Do it now so you don't forget!

# PART 5

# GETTING LINKS TO YOUR SITE AND BUILDING YOUR WEB PRESENCE

Off-Page Search Engine Optimization: What you do elsewhere on the internet to help boost visitors and gain credibility in the eyes of Google. For this you need links and brand mentions for your site.

I continue to implement all the techniques mentioned here for clients. They do work.

It's important that you implement many of these tips gradually as opposed to just spending a week building thousands of links and then not doing anything at all. Slow and steady wins the race in this field.

Let's dive in.

## How To Nail Google My Business, Bing Places And Yahoo Local

You may have heard of Google Places or Google Local before - this is now called Google My Business. Microsoft has their own version called Bing Places which is also worth setting up as Bing's market share is rising.

Here's some tips, focusing more on Google:

1. Whatever you do, don't rely on Google My Business to keep your business afloat. Sure, you might have a nice ranking today….

If Google were a child it would be diagnosed with ADD. Everything just has to change. All the time. Without stopping.

(*Author's note: within 48 hours of writing the above, Google released a major change to their search engine affecting Google My Business.)

2. Ensure that your details are correctly listed everywhere on all directories and websites. If Google gets confused as to the details of your website, it'll hurt your rankings. This means that if you change location, you need to go back and find all the places you listed yourself and update those details.

3. Encourage people to leave reviews. This isn't a magic pill to success but is an effective method to help you. It needs to be an ongoing process, too. Google is maddeningly

inconsistent with this but businesses receiving more reviews are more likely to rank better.

4. Get your phone number and/or address mentioned all over the place, alongside your business name. Google looks for mentions of your business around the internet and this plays a part in helping you get rankings. These mentions are known as local citations, and help a bunch ranking in Google.

5. Link to your listing from your website.

6. Verify Your Listing. It's crucially important to verify your listing as fast as possible. It's normally a phone call but Google may well send you a postcard with a pin code. Tell your staff to keep an eye out as that postcard is worth big money to your business. It's mind-blowing how many times staff members just throw this stuff in the garbage as if it's junk mail. Communicate to your staff the importance of this card.

7. Input as much information as you can. Opening hours, contact details, payment methods accepted, your website. Go as far as possible.

8. Upload a stack of photos. Listings with more photos get more engagement.

9. Don't spam your listing with keywords. This is the quickest way to end up at the bottom of the Google pile – they hate it when local businesses try to spam their profile with keywords, so just don't do it. You can, however, put a little bit of juice in your description. "We offer Pizza Walking Tours in San Francisco CA" is acceptable as a sentence. Just make your listing appear natural.

10. Design a cover image. As with all social profiles, it's always worth having a cover image designed just for your Google Plus profile.

## How To Get Your Listings On Other Websites To Rank Highly In Google

To get visitors to your site, you don't just need to get your website or Google My Business listing to be #1 in the search results. Other listings you have around the internet can rank highly on their own and help you get customers on their own.

TripAdvisor, Yelp and other websites have a lot of power in Google, meaning you could get your listings on these sites into the top ten for various searches. Imagine if you had your website at number one, and then the next few search results were your TripAdvisor and Yelp listings? That's powerful stuff.

Here's three basic tips to make this happen:

1. When you input your business name on your listing is descriptive. For example, Bob's Walking Tours gives Google nothing. Bob's Walking Tours New York will work much better and also feels natural. This increases your chances of local directories accepting your listing compared to those who try to jam their business title with SEO keywords such as 'Bob's Walking Tours New York | Bob's Tours NYC'

2. Write a detailed listing using specific words related to your tour as opposed to banalities such as 'we pride ourselves on service' (who doesn't pride themselves on service?).

3. Link to all your main listings from the home page of your website to give them an extra little boost in their Google rankings. The links don't need to be right up the top – put them anywhere.

Remember, if your website can't get into the top 5, at least your listing might be able to.

## List Yourself In WikiTravel and WikiVoyage

WikiTravel is a fantastic place to generate some extra business. WikiVoyage is also growing and worth looking at.

These two websites are editable online encyclopedias, much like Wikipedia except with a focus on travel advice (Wikivoyage is a sub-project of Wikipedia itself). No matter where you are, they'll have a page for your area. The best thing? Anyone can edit them.

You can edit any page and add your business as a listing but it's often too obvious when a tourism business edits a page to praise themselves. Try at the very least to make your listing appear neutral and add other businesses (non-competitors of yours) to the page and some other information to make it look like you're not just editing these pages for your exclusive benefit.

Try not to delete other businesses from those pages either. It's just poor form and could lead to an edit war where you and someone else spend all your time deleting each other's mentions.

This method is an easy way to list yourself in a high traffic website - for free!

## Go Bonkers Submitting Your Site To Directories

Submitting to local directories may well give you a big boost in Google. If you're a local business you can get helped just by mentions of your business name without even getting a link, known as local citations.

The entire process below is offered as a service by us but if you want to go it alone, here's a few tips:

1. Build a gigantic list of local directories (and other relevant directories) and submit to a few each month, starting with the most important ones. Start by Googling "tour operator directories" or "New York tour operators" and things like that.

2. To get this list, turn to Google. Start by Googling for tour related terms and go to pages 4, 5, 6, 20, 30 to find websites with listings.

3. Google the business name of multiple other local tourism businesses to find out where they are listed. Go to pages 10, 20.

4. Google the web address of other local tourism businesses - you'll often find some gems here that the previous tips didn't discover.

5. Check out major tourism cities or regions elsewhere in the world and Google a few of their business names and web addresses. Chances are you'll find some opportunities there that local competitors are overlooking.

6. Look for travel directories that are relevant to your niche.

7. Are you a member of a minority, cultural or ethnic group? For example, you may be from India but operate in Australia: there is a directory of Indian-run businesses in Australia.

8. Get a link from any business associations you're a member of. Better Business Bureau, local tourism associations and more.

9. Close this out by using tools. Whitespark.ca and Bright Local are the two best. They enable you to ferret out listings of other tour businesses that you hadn't yet found. Why do I advocate doing this last? These tools are hit and miss and as such are best used as a final clean-up.

Resources:

Whitespark.ca/local-citation-finder

Brightlocal.com

## Have A Blog? Get Some Great Links For Your Site

Starting a blog and putting 10 (or even 5) posts up there is a good idea because you can then use that blog to get your site listed in many places that other operators would never even have submitted.

The key is to make sure your blog is a genuine resource of information for travelers to your area as opposed to a pitch fest.

Here's some tips.

a) Conduct searches for things like "blog directories" and "blog directory lists" to turn up a large quantity of potential places to submit.

b) Google "travel blog directory", "travel blog directories" and "travel blog links" and you'll find many options.

c) Google this:

intitle:travel blog inurl:"links" OR "resources"

and Google this:

intitle:tours inurl:"links" OR "resources"

The above text is a special way to use Google to find additional resources that will link to your site.

Also try this:

intitle:travel blog links

d) If you're a member of a minority, ethnic or cultural group you can get links from within your sphere. As an example, a Chinese business newspaper might want to report on the success of a Chinese resident in Los Angeles.

## An Easy Trick To Find The Links Of Other Tourism Businesses In Your Area (And Elsewhere)

By now, you're doing great. I bet we can find more potential links for you however.

There now exist some brilliant tools that dig up the links of your competition and pretty much any other website you care to mention.

Check out Ahrefs.com All you have to do is input the URL of your competitor's business and that's it. Boom. You can now see all the different websites around the world that are linking to your competitor's site. From there you can then visit the websites your competitors are listed on and try to get a link there too.

Getting the same links as your competitors is great, but there's more. You'll generate a lot of marketing ideas too as you'll find your competition doing things you had no idea about.

Previously, I've conducted competitor research where ALL the businesses in a niche each using a different tactic to build links. For my client, we just cherry-picked the links that many of their competitors had built and ended up with a market-dominating campaign.

Many of you reading this won't have much competition or you may not have much competition that's active on the internet. Go look at what people are doing in major cities or similar (but larger) tourism destinations to yours.

The tool I used to recommend in times past was Ahrefs.com but for smaller businesses, SEMCompass.com will work just fine as it gives you limited access to the database of Ahrefs.com. Unless you're working on some major $$$$ campaigns, you won't even notice the limits.

## Jump In Bed With Local Bloggers, Travel Bloggers, Online Guides And Local Tourism Businesses That Also Have Blogs

Building relationships with bloggers in your niche has always been something that is simple and beneficial, regardless of who you are.

Here's a few tips for dealing with local bloggers to maximize the potential of a great relationship with them:

1. Don't be a taker. For the love of whatever is holy, don't ask something from a blogger in your first interaction. Focus on the relationship.

2. Try to make their lives better. Most bloggers are incessantly emailed by people looking to get links from them or or even worse, from people who spam them with offers. Try not to be that girl or guy.

3. Go to local meet-ups you know bloggers will be at and make that the first step of the relationship building process. To find local meet-ups, search on Facebook for local expat, tourism or blogger communities. There's also Couchsurfing.org and Meetup.com, which both have regular meet-ups

4. Offer to write a guest post for their blog on a topic of your specialty once you have an established relationship. They get a great blog post, you get the link.

5. Offer them photos from your operation royalty-free.

A big irritation for bloggers is that it's tough to get their hands on royalty-free photography – annoyingly hard. Just tell them to take any photo off of your site or Facebook when needed and in return, ask for a link as credit.

Some will take you up on it, others won't, but it's a nice offer to make.

6. Offer giveaways through their site. A lot of bloggers enjoy giveaways as it gives them the chance to give something back to their readers, who will enjoy taking part.

7. Offer them a free tour - it will help them generate content for their blog. Outside of peak season is when you have more capacity and it's time to take advantage of this. Every empty seat on a tour is a wasted PR opportunity.

They don't even need to be dedicated travel bloggers. If they live in your area and have a blog, that's enough. Remember, the cost of putting someone in an empty seat is next to nothing.

8. Create an affiliate program for local websites. TourCMS is an example of booking software with the capability to reward people for every time they send a sale through to you, so you can have a productive commercial relationship tied to the amount of revenue they generate for you.

9. Be wary of sponsoring local blogs on an ongoing basis. It's rare to see a situation where sponsorship that's not tied to an actual return on investment works out.

10. Allow them to sell your tours on their site. You could even sell tours directly through a page on their own website, where they receive a commission on each sale.

## RUN AN EVENT FOR BLOGGERS

As above, it's nice to invite bloggers onto your tours to fill empty seats in non-peak times. I would recommend this in the case of bloggers that aren't the biggest players in your area. There's local bloggers and then there are the sites that show up every time someone runs a Google search for information about your region. Those bloggers need to be treated like the precious resource they are.

Create a specific trip or event just for this group of prominent website owners and bloggers.

There's two types of events you can run:

Event Idea 1: Free Tour

Depending on your capacity, invite 5, 10 or more bloggers down and make an event. Bloggers enjoy hanging out with other bloggers. You'll even find that a lot of them already know each other.

Not only this, you can spend your whole time focusing on them, building relationships and trying to generate potential ongoing partnerships.

If you do this, focus on making sure they have a great tour experience - obviously - but in the down times of the tour, ask them questions about online marketing and how they normally work with operators. Seek to learn their world and how it works.

Event Idea 2: An Industry Meet and Greet

This would be a bit of an exercise but the payoff could be

massive and hey, it'd be a lot of fun.

With this idea, you create an event at a local venue, get many bloggers and website owners down and lots of people from your industry along for the ride, too. Just make it a simple meet and greet where the focus is more on people standing and mingling than sitting.

It's mutually beneficial for everyone which is a great key to successful events. Not only that, it'd be easy to win the support of your local tourism organization to help promote it.

## Require A Link From Suppliers

Always be aware of situations where you could potentially get a link.

A fantastic possibility is to require a link from all suppliers. Just say to your salesperson "Look, I want to buy this, but on one condition: that you create a link to my website featuring me as a happy customer or in your testimonials with a link back to my site."

Your supplier may never have heard this before but it's an entirely reasonable request and one that also benefits them because they get a full testimonial on their site which helps them generate more sales.

You can try this with basically any purchase that involves contact with a salesperson. I know that with our service, we would be MORE than happy to provide a back-link to anyone who gives us a testimonial.

# Hiring An SEO Company: The 3 Things You Need To Avoid

(As a reminder, SEO stands for Search Engine Optimization, and it's the process of making your website appear higher in relevant Google search results.)

1. Vague action plans. Many SEO Companies refuse to be specific in terms of the plan they put together and the work they do. This is rubbish. Whatever 'reasons' they offer, do not listen to them. You need to be able evaluate their methods before you risk your hard-earned Quetzales.

2. Quitting too early. Doing SEO is like growing a plant - you need to water it. If you expect your plant to flourish without going through the proper process... You're crazy. Same thing with SEO.

3. Signing a long-term contract. There's no good business reason that an SEO company needs to sign a long-term contract. There just isn't. If their model requires a long-term contract, they should be changing their model. If they do a lot of up-front work, pay for it up-front instead of loading it out over 24 months.

Doing SEO is a time-expensive exercise and as a result, it should appear expensive to you. If it seems cheap or affordable, it's a good sign that you should be running the other way. Fast.

Dodgy SEO practices can lead to an automatic penalty which can then tank your traffic overnight. I've seen this happen countless times. It's not worth the risk.

# PART 6

# HOW TO CRUSH IT WITH VIDEO

You're already aware that YouTube is a pretty big deal (... I hope!) You're also most likely aware that making a video can be a difficult exercise.

Just one great video can have a big shift on sales. In fact, you're pretty much guaranteed to get major returns on a good video. For this reason, if your business is serious for you - and not a part-time thing - you should put this on your to do list.

## Why Video Matters So Much

1. Video is a big deal. Did you know that YouTube is the world's second biggest search engine (after Google)? You know people love watching video but you may be surprised just how much people love it.

2. It increases your online presence. Having even just the one marketing video on YouTube gives people an additional way discover you, with the added bonus that Google often ranks videos right up there.

3. It connects with people emotionally. Have you ever noticed how much more a video that's even just 5 seconds will capture the personality of a loved one, compared to a photo? That connection will make people far more likely to book with you.

4. Video stays with people and causes them to remember you over all others. Whenever I see a small business using video, I find that the video returns to my memory several times over the days that follow. Getting memorability like that without video is super tough.

5. It allows people to pre-experience your tour. With a video, your service goes from being a vague idea to being a specific concept sitting there right in front of them. It's at the core of why video succeeds.

Human beings are simply not built to deal in the abstract. Even if they understand that you do bus trips to the forest, it won't feel real to them until they experience it. You become a known quantity against the unknown which gives you a huge leg-up on your competition.

6. Your guests want video. Not convinced yet by the previous points? How's about this: according to a study of retail websites conducted by Comscore, after watching a video people stay on a website for an average of 2 minutes longer and are 64% more likely to purchase. In my own experience, whenever businesses add a great video to their site they get a bump.

7. TripAdvisor now lets you upload your video. What a great way to stick out from the pack.

# Tips To Make A Great Promo Video

1. Use people who know what they're doing. If you're on a super tight budget and handy with a computer, at least make sure you have a decent camera, a good microphone and a tripod.

2. Start with a plan. Before shooting the first frame, there needs to be a clear idea of exactly which words you will say and what shots you (or the video person) will take.

3. Inject some humor into your script. Making people smile can never hurt.

4. Make it feel personal. People want to deal with people, not businesses.

5. Focus on two things: the experience and what makes you the best at delivering it.

6. Keep it short. 60 seconds - 90 seconds works just to give people a basic taste as to who you are and what you do.

7. Feature happy customers if you like... just don't point the camera and tell them to "say something." It's desperately painful to watch business promo videos where a customer is looking at the camera scratching to think of what they should be saying. Ask them a question like "how's the trip going?" or "so what's your favorite thing about Giraffe Tours?" This gives them the cue to say something short and snappy.

8. Keep filming to the early morning or late afternoon

where possible. The light looks better and there's a lot less squinting into the sun.

9. Be super mindful of the audio. The quickest way to film a useless video is to have bad sound. I'm saying this from hard-won experience.

I once used a guy who seemed like a pro with his nice camera, nice lights and nice microphones. Just one problem: it was his first time using that particular microphone. The video was wrecked because the sound was terrible and we had to start over again a week later.

Stay out of the wind and make sure you continuously are checking the sound quality by listening back to the videos. The best case scenario is to use a lapel microphone which is less likely to have issues.

Now You Have a Great Video, Put That Thing Up in LIGHTS!

Video should always be in one place on your site: at the top and in the middle.

The #1 goal of any website that has a video needs to be to make people watch that video.

It will be be your biggest sales weapon. Use it fully.

## Making A Great Video On A Budget

With a bit of lateral thinking, it's simple to cut video production costs in half. I've successfully followed the exact process below.

1. The biggest key to saving money is to unbundle the costs. You don't have to use the same person to film and edit.

2. Find a freelance videographer using local networks. You don't need a video agency or ad agency. Those nice offices? They're paid for by you. Many freelancers are great at what they do but charge more competitively.

3. Check out ProductionHub.com, which has a massive directory full of video pros. Also have a look at Videopixie or Viedit. Alternate sources can be Craigslist, Gumtree or local college/university job boards.

4. Find a video editor online using a service like oDesk and upload the videos to them using a service such as Dropbox. The key with oDesk is to make a private job ad and then search for people who have great reviews on their profile. Look for people with a rating of 4.9/5 or higher. Show them videos you like and be very specific in describing your needs.

## VIDEO TESTIMONIALS

Nowadays it's easy and cheap for you to have a basic video camera with you at all times. For most people this will be a smartphone, a FlipHD or GoPro. All those options are fine.

Get your camera out during down times or towards the end of a tour and ask them if you can take a short video. Just say "Hey, is it OK to take a quick video to put on my site? It's super simple - I just ask you 3 basic questions, it takes 30 seconds."

Here's the three basic questions you can ask all people:

1. Hey, what do you think of Portland?
2. What's been your favorite part of this trip?
3. What would you say to people who are still considering whether to go or not?

Using this approach will be more helpful because your guest isn't floundering in front of the camera wondering what to say. Get a few on your site and it will help you win more business.

# START A YOUTUBE CHANNEL

A little earlier in this book you saw how easy it is to come up with blog post ideas.

It is a fair amount more effort to make videos instead of blog posts, but WAY more powerful. A video blog will get you a LOT more visibility from Google and as mentioned before, will make it easier for you to connect with your guests on a human level.

For an example of a successful YouTube channel, check out "Sean ResortRebel". It's a simple hotel in the Philippines that has amassed 1.5 million views just by uploading a ton of videos on a consistent basis and trying to have a bit of fun with it all. Honestly, some of the videos are downright creepy (just in terms of the channel's attitude towards women) but it doesn't seem to have affected his success.

Your chances of success are hugely increased compared to a normal text blog. There's so many people using YouTube and it's so easy to get videos ranked highly in Google right now that if you consistently upload video and get the basics of light and video right, it's basically impossible to fail. The same cannot be said at all of blogs.

I've listed here a few tips to making that video blog a success. For more comprehensive guides, go to YouTube and (surprise surprise!) you'll find a wealth of videos about making a successful channel.

<u>1. Make videos about stuff that people are searching for.</u>
Think back to the keyword research earlier in this book and blog post ideas.

How does one get from the airport to the city late at night when the train is no longer running? That's a common question that very few bloggers answer in their cute 'How To Get to Barcelona Airport' posts.

Also do general tips videos – such as 'the top 9 places to eat during your stay in Oslo'. Focus on sharing lots of great information about your area. Think about the sort of information you need when you travel.

<u>2. Give each video a descriptive title AND a detailed description.</u> This will majorly help your video attract visits through Google and relevant videos in YouTube. When someone is watching a video in YouTube, there will often be other similar videos on the right hand side to watch next. You want to appear there.

<u>3. As before, make good use of the description area.</u> Write with detail and put a link back to your site – although please note that the link has zero SEO value. Use it to not only summarize your video but be sure to include – in a non-spammy way – keywords that are relevant to the video.

<u>4. Be patient.</u> The views come in time.

<u>5. Use a tripod to keep your camera stable.</u> Nothing is more distracting than watching a video with a camera person desperately trying to keep their hand stable.

<u>6. To avoid sound issues, stand nice and close to the camera.</u> Stand (a lot) closer than you think is natural because your instincts are most likely wrong. Only your upper chest and head needs to be visible. One of the biggest mistakes made by beginners is to stand quite a few yards away from the camera so that their entire body can be seen. This is

completely unnecessary and looks silly. If you can see your belt in the video, step in one yard closer.

Especially if outside, make sure to use a shotgun or lapel (AKA 'lavalier') microphone to keep sound quality high. Shotgun microphones are long and thin and want you typically see used by movies and TV crews. A lapel mic is that which you pin to your shirt and it will boost the quality of your audio way up.

7. Use annotations. Video annotations are those little boxes that show up during YouTube videos. Make good use of these to get people subscribing to your channel or clicking other links as they really do work to get a watcher's attention. If part of a video has gone out of date, you can add annotations to the video to give people the correct info.

8. Link your official channel to your site in the channel admin area. Make use of this. You can also put in links to your social media channels on the home page of your YouTube channel.

9. Seek to drive action with every video. I'd recommend to close with a basic call to action getting people to go to your site. It helps a lot if you have something to attract people to your site, such as a free guide to your city as mentioned before.

10. Do sell in all videos, but keep it light. Start with your name, your company and a 5-10 word rundown of what you do.

11. Embed your videos in a blog post every time instead of just leaving YouTube to show it to people. It's way better to have a blog post with the video on your own site showing

up in Google's results than just the video on YouTube This way, you can get people to subscribe to your free guide or your mailing list beneath the video or simply encourage them to keep navigating the site.

12. Use any camera besides your web cam The sound and video quality of web cams is nearly always terrible which makes your videos unwatchable.

13. Watch your lighting. Lighting really, really matters and will be make the difference for how long people stick around. You'd be surprised how cheap a basic lighting kit could be to have decent lighting! On Amazon, lighting kits can run as low as $120. Sunlight also works fantastically well, just make sure you don't have the sun pointing into your eyes.

Filming on location can be a great idea which means you don't have to worry about light - just remember my advice to avoid filming in the middle of the day to avoid harsh light and squinting. Being outside does create sound issues as well so you need to be highly mindful of this. Stay out of the wind – even a gentle breeze can wreck a video – and stand nice and close to the camera.

14. Keep most videos short and sweet. 1-5 minutes is perfectly fine.

15. Create a few 'pillar' videos that offer more value. We use the word pillar because pillars hold up a building - or in this case, they keep your video strategy standing tall. This where you unload a decent amount of tips such as "15 Tips For an Amazing Stay in Amsterdam" "My Top 5 'Hidden Secret' Restaurants in Paris" "The 8 Incredible Places ALL

Visitors to South Africa NEED To Know About".

Put more effort into these ones as you'll be driving visitors to them. At the end of the video, spend some time at the end pushing people to your website. Don't be afraid at the end of these videos of using a hard sell - if they stop watching without having heard why you're amazing, they're lost to you anyway.

<u>16. Use video thumbnails at the end of each video.</u> This drives people to watch other videos on your channel.

<u>17. Spend a little bit of money on getting things right and use a semi-decent camera</u>. $500 should be enough to buy something that will kick some real goals for you. You don't need to spend $5000 on a studio. The camera we use for our own YouTube channel – the Nikon D3200 – cost me around $500 and it works great.

<u>18. Your videos have one ultimate goal: to make a sale.</u> Because of this, it's important to maintain this front of mind and ensure that everything is about getting people to know you, like you or trust you – the three key components for earning clients.

<u>19. Keep the pace up</u>. One of the biggest errors by newbie You Tubers is that they have a wandering style and you're just wanting them to get to the bleeping point! You need to be concise and use editing to cut out all dead moments.

# PART 7

# HOW TO MAKE PAID ONLINE MARKETING WORK FOR YOU

> "A man who stops advertising to save money is like a man who stops a clock to save time" – Henry Ford.

A little while ago I was chatting to a tour operator who told me proudly: "I've never spent a cent on marketing."

This operator in particular relied on his top 5 ranking on TripAdvisor for 80% of his business in a city with 300 competitors. Just one or two bad reviews could send him to number 35 on that list (and bankruptcy court!) The amount of times I've seen a business suddenly tumble from the top 10 is ridiculous and I don't want it to happen to you either.

Why would you strangle the growth of your business because of an obsession with using only free marketing sources? I feel strongly about this because I have seen too many businesses tank because of a stubborn persistence with free methods only.

Because of this, one of the best methods to guarantee ongoing sustainability is to include paid marketing sources in your mix. This counts even if you're selling out every day – at the least use paid marketing to fill up seats on the edge dates of your seasons.

Successfully using paid marketing at least to some extent makes you much more defensible against the random shocks that can hit businesses - from a negative TripAdvisor Review which takes you down the rankings to a Google update which knocks your site back to page 4.

# Retargeting: The Almost-Free Marketing Method Which Puts You In Front Of Thousands

Imagine being able to advertise to thousands of people.. all of them interested in your service... for almost free.

Even if you're the most reluctant person in the world to use money on marketing, this method is very cheap and one of the few marketing methods that I would recommend to literally anyone.

So, what is this magical pixie dust?

Retargeting, or as Google would have us call it, remarketing. It's simple and beautiful: a visitor comes to your website, leaves and then starts seeing ads around the internet and on Facebook for your business reminding them of your service. What's more, these ads are cheap.

In my experience the cost the cost is around $3 for 1000 impressions around the general internet but more on Facebook. This is marketing gold. Now you can reach the people who visited your website but for whatever reason didn't book in that exact moment – otherwise known as the EXACT people you want to be advertising to – and you pay peanuts for it.

A cookie is 'dropped' on to the visitor's computer and for the next 30, 60 or 90 days they will see ads for your service.

It's fairly simple to implement and manage (well, for me

at least) but if you don't want the hassle, there are many companies that do it for you including mine.

Rather than setting up individual accounts with Google and Facebook, campaigns can be created using 3rd-party services such as Adroll or PerfectAudience. Go and try it yourself! Facebook also has their own system which is scarily good.

Banners can be made using your design agency or freelancers at places such as Envato Studio, Freelancer, oDesk, Elance or even Fiverr.com. You can even have a try at doing it yourself using Canva.com.

## VIDEO RETARGETING

We've already taken a look at normal retargeting, where you display ads around the internet to people who have visited your website. Step two: if you have a great new promo video now after reading this book you can also make use of it for video retargeting. It's a great opportunity to make that video work a lot harder for you – you can advertise to people for almost free with it.

If you use YouTube – and let's be honest here, you do - you will have noticed the video ads that play before and during videos.

YouTube doesn't charge you if the person watches thirty seconds or less of your video which means that in many cases, people are being reminded of your business even as they skip your ad. Now, THAT is winning.

Aside from showing video ads to people who have visited your website, you can also show video ads to people who have viewed other videos on your Youtube channel. Go to our Youtube channel – named Tourism Tiger – and watch a video to see it in action.

## Include Call To Actions In All Of Your Ads And Banners

A call to action is where you make known to a user what action you would like them to take.

In most online ads, this will be a graphical button that is designed as part of the banner. The entire banner is clickable, but the appearance of a button will cause more people to click it. For example a button with text specifying what action will happen such as "View Tours" or "Book Your Trip Now" will generate more clicks.

Typical ads that don't have a very specific action needed from a user will often fail (or at least get less clicks) because they assume the user knows what is expected of them. Assumptions like this are false! Most users on the internet (including you) are on autopilot and often need a small nudge to knock them out of it.

## MAKE USE OF FACEBOOK'S PAID SERVICES TO PUSH YOUR OFFERS TO YOUR FANS

Facebook has nearly completely strangled the ability of businesses to interact for free with people who like their page. Where a post you made might have been seen by 20% of your fans previously, now that figure has dropped to below 10%, if not 5%. That's super low and the idea is to make it so you pay money to get your posts back in front of users.

The reason for this change is that Facebook's own data was showing that people were getting sick of businesses jamming their news feeds with constant promotion. When people use Facebook they generally are there to read funny things, get engaged in political debates or interact with their friends – not read about the latest special from Charlotte's Flowers.

Happily – for Facebook's investors at least – there's still a way to get back in front of your fans. You can pay to 'boost' your post and put yourself in front of the people who have said that they want to hear from you.

It really is great value. Do it and set the budget low just as an experiment. Just by paying $10-20 you'll find that there's a good chance nearly your entire list will see the post (unless you have many thousands of fans, in which case you will have to pay a little more). It's an affordable way to maintain the attention of the people who want to hear from you.

Many operators resent this and don't want to pay money to talk to their page's fans. Unfortunately, that's life and that's business. Wherever there's return on investment to be had, go for it!

## Hire A Professional To Manage Paid Advertising

They say that there's a great way to make $1000 from paid advertising - that's to start with $10,000! While an SEO campaign can feasibly be run by yourself if you really get into it – and after you've used a professional to verify your setup – an Adwords campaign will be tougher. As such, I always recommend using a specialist. That being said, it's still worth learning the basic mechanics of how Google Adwords works.

Google provides their own employees to help and advise you on your campaigns but - how do I say this - they are about as useful as a ski jacket in the Sahara Desert.

In my agency, we use a specialist. If you can't afford a specialist on an ongoing basis, at the very least consider paying a professional to get your campaign going for the first few months and then do a regular audit. If you're not using a specialist, you should be checking in on your account on a minimum weekly basis.

Alternatively, there are platforms such as Trada and oDesk where you can find Adwords professionals. These are great but it's better to use a tourism specialist, simply because you can benefit from the lessons learned managing other people's campaigns.

## You Will Always Lose Money on Adwords First Up - The Key Is To Persist

In my online marketing career, the amount of companies I have seen that have made money from their first few months of an Adwords campaign is few and far and between.

You know what? This is fantastic. You might think it's a drag to have to go through several months of losing money on Adwords but you can trust me that it's the best thing possible.

Why?

1. Your competitors will not persist. Most small businesses give up on Adwords after one or two months after not being able to point to any positive results. This means that once you break even on your campaigns you've joined the exclusive club of businesses that can generate money from Pay Per Click marketing. This will give you a massive leg-up as you work to fill empty spots on tours.

2. There are few things that will improve your business more than losing money on Adwords. This is because there's two basic reasons you're losing money on your campaign – either it's not optimized in the right way OR your website needs improving. This is where the gold is: improving your website doesn't benefit you just for Adwords, it helps you across the board and will help you increase sales to visitors coming from ALL traffic sources.

The first month of an ad campaign tends to be atrocious. I have a client who charges around $350 for a day tour. In her campaign's first month, it cost around $750 of ads to generate each booking. The next month, it cost $190 of ads per booking. The next month, it cost $90 to generate each conversion and she was making a very healthy profit from her campaign! It's worth investing the money and losing some up-front because if you can turn this thing profitable, it's like having a cash machine. Just spin it up and begin to add money to your bank account.

Create ads for specific tours and keywords then send clicks directly to the relevant pages for those ads, which in most cases will NOT be the home page.

## Adwords: A Basic Explanation

The first step to success on Adwords is understanding how it works. Like Google's search engine, it has grown more and more complex but I believe it is still within your reach if you really, truly dedicate yourself to learning the platform. That being said, it's fairly easy to write a 300 page book on this topic and still leave a lot out.

Before I dive in, please know that using Adwords will not help your rankings in the normal search results in Google. Anyone who tells you otherwise is 100% incorrect.

Adwords is an auction system. Every time someone searches for something, Google runs an auction between ads and the auction winner gets displayed on top. Be aware that the amount of money you bid is just one factor in this equation. Google will show the ad that is most likely to make them money, not just the one that bids the highest.

Just like with any other online campaign, you'll do better with Adwords if you align yourself to Google's financial incentives.

If your ad gets more clicks than the next one, Google will give you a higher position for your ad even if you bid lower. The math is simple: 10 clicks at $3 a click is more valuable than 2 clicks at $8 a click. Your initial and ongoing focus needs to be on doing everything you can to get more clicks. This means more money for Google and cheaper clicks for you.

If all else being equal, you bid $10 and the next guy down bids $6, what would happen? Will Google take your

$10, despite the next bid being a lot lower? No. Google determines the price of your click based on the person who bid the next highest amount to ensure that top bidders don't get ripped off. In that sense it's almost like an auction in real life – the top bidder only pays the highest amount that the second highest bidder was willing to pay.

The BIGGEST thing however that will impact on the success of your Adwords campaign is not the Adwords campaign itself – it's the quality of the website that you're sending your visitors to. Fix your website first (details coming later in this book) and then focus on Adwords.

Let's take a look at some of the basic terms:

CPC - Cost per click. How much you pay each time someone clicks.

CTR - Click through rate. What percentage of people click on your ad after seeing it.

CPA - Cost per action. How much it costs you to drive a certain action – be that an inquiry or a sale. Also referred to as cost per acquisition.

Quality Score - Google's measure of the quality of your campaign, including the actual website you're attempting to send people to. In Google's words: "expected click through rate, ad relevance, and landing page experience "

Ad Rank - Google's definition: "Your Ad Rank is a score that's based on your bid, the components of Quality Score and the expected impact of extensions and other ad formats. " On a basic level you can use this formula: Ad Rank = Quality Score x Bid.

Negative Keyword - Keywords that you don't want Google to show your ads for.

Impression Share - The percentage of times Google has shown your ad for a particular search.

Landing Page - Where the visitor is directed to after clicking on an ad.

## Adwords: Dedicate Time And Energy To Mobile

Make sure you have a great mobile experience on your site if you're going to be using Adwords. In fact, just make sure you have a great mobile experience on your site full stop.

With mobile devices including iPads now around 50% of all search traffic and growing fast, you're going to be wasting a BOATLOAD of money on your campaigns if you don't have a fantastic experience ready for those people arriving to your site.

Here's the tips:

1. Track conversions, bounce rate and average time on site on mobile - tracking conversions on mobile is something that is not particularly difficult and will give you some great insights. Is your site performing better or worse on mobile? Why? If you're already tracking conversions, Google Analytics automatically tracks the sales you make on mobile – you'll just need to dig a little into their site to make it happen.

2. Use the mobile bid adjuster – Google gives you the ability to adjust your bids up and down for mobile devices – you can drop the bids down to zero (or in Google's terminology, negative 100%) or you can raise them 300%. Your mobile site, for better or worse, will not convert at exactly the same rate as your desktop site. Make good use of the mobile bid adjuster to ensure that you're getting acceptable levels of return on smaller devices.

3. Show different ads on mobile – there's little probability that the same ads will perform the same way on desktop and mobile. Add a little bit of variation spice to that mix and track the difference.

4. Enable click-to-call – Google has now enabled a function where you can have people on mobile click a button inside the ad and immediately call you. Keep this in mind if you do a lot of of business over the phone.

5. Consider turning mobile ads off. In some cases, Adwords traffic that comes through mobile just doesn't work. In that scenario there'll be no choice but to turn it off by dialing bids down 100% on mobile. You could have a crappy mobile site, a terrible mobile booking experience or visitors on their phones could simply be in a different mood. If you're not prepared to spend your way to success with mobile you'll break my heart here but sometimes it must be done: turn it off.

# ADWORDS: ANALYZE PERFORMANCE FOR DAYS OF THE WEEK & SEASONS

If you're running Adwords campaigns you should keep a close eye on the variation of your performance in terms of days of the week.

Some day tour operators especially can see major variance in terms of which days perform better for them. I've seen one tour operator whose conversions TANKED on the weekend which is when the tours were running. People were coming to the site and realizing that they had missed out for that weekend and in most cases weren't coming back again.

You may also find that your campaigns perform better for you in peak season compared to shoulder season (or even vice versa). There's just no way to know without tracking and testing.

Matthew Newton

# ADWORDS: IMPROVING YOUR QUALITY SCORE

If you want to be successful on Google Adwords, it's imperative that you focus on Quality Score. The higher your Quality Score is, the less you need to bid to get to the same position!

Google introduced Quality Score in 2005 to combat a wave of spammy activity that was occurring on the Adwords platform. Google's main source of profits is Adwords, which means they're very sensitive about protecting the quality of the ads they display.

As long as ads remain relevant, people will keep clicking. If they allow low-quality ads, Google may experience a short-term increase in revenue but over time less and less people will click. The idea is that Google can make more money for years to come.

Quality Score is applied at all levels: the account , Ad Group, keyword and the actual ad. Your entire history on Adwords also has an effect on your Quality Score, too, so new accounts will often find themselves at a disadvantage.

A mix of the relevance of your ad, the expected Click Through Rate and the experience the user has when they hit your website will determine your QS. Your landing page experience is based on three things: having great, relevant content, having a website that is easy to navigate, and the transparency of your offering. Google will even look at you perform in the geographic region of the person who is clicking and what device they are using.

Here's a few tips for improving your Quality Score:

1. Maintain a great account structure. This is the first and most important step to getting and keeping a high Quality Score. Make sure your Ad Groups small stay and on theme. Keep things super relevant without targeting too many keywords in a group. Part of your Quality Score is determined by how many clicks Google thinks your ad will get based on past performance before they see your actual CTR. Every time you put the effort in to create a great ad, you're not just investing in that ad, you're investing in the future of your account.

2. Write specific ad copy for each Ad Group. Relevance is everything and Click-Through Rate is a big measure of this – that's why we'll talk about how to improve CTR in just a minute.

3. Create specific landing pages for each Ad Group instead of sending all visitors to the home page. This helps to keep ads relevant.

4. Always have at least two ads running to develop your instincts as to what works and what doesn't. Test, test, test. Adwords is a game and if you play it, you will increase your chances of success.

5. Gear your landing pages to the ads you're showing. We need to see nice consistency between the ad and your website – if your ad is about winery tours and the page you're sending visitors to is about winery tours, Google will love you. As before, relevance is key!

6. Don't bother trying to optimize ads/keywords that receive few impressions, beyond your initial efforts – the

QS they receive is based on the overall account score. You can spend all day long trying to improve their QS and it will not budge. To increase impressions and make the ads receive their own QS, you can switch from exact match to phrase match or relax the themes of the ads so that they're not too tightly focused.

7. Make improvements to your landing page. Google wants to send people to great websites, therefore your site needs to be built well. It must load fast, work well on mobile and have lots of content.

8. Include a privacy policy on your site. This comes back to transparency, which I mentioned earlier. As a business which is taking bookings, Google wants to see you protecting the privacy of your visitors.

9. Improve your Click-Through Rate. Just by having ads that people are more likely to click on, Google will give you a better Quality Score. In just one short moment, I'll give you a guide on how to do this.

10. Pay someone to have a look at your account. If you don't want an Adwords professional ongoing this could be a very expensive mistake, but at the very least pay someone to do an audit for you.

11. Keep geographic performance in mind, as this forms part of your assessment. What countries or areas typically provide you the best business? Without a doubt, these areas will be the ones that generate the best performance for you on Adwords.

12. Try to understand that QS is just one part of the picture – your focus is on making money and if an ad with low QS

*Sell More Tours*

is making you money but you're unable to raise it... Who cares?

# Adwords – Raising Click-Through Rate (CTR)

For mine, increasing Click Through Rate (CTR) is what you should spend most time You'll get more clicks at lower bids, greatly increasing the chances of a profitable campaign.

Here's the tips for increasing CTR:

1. Write ads for keywords. A basic rule of PPC is that the ad that best matches the word someone is searching for (and thereby, their intent) is the ad that will win. It also helps a lot that Google bolds the keywords in your ad which match what the user has searched for.

2. Test, test, test. Don't test just small variations – make ads with wildly different copy in them and then see what happens. Be boring, be salesy, be funny, be controversial. It's impossible to predict which ad will win, but over time you'll find that your ability to write better ads improves.

3. Analyze ads for similar businesses in different markets. By analyze, I mean, of course, that you should 'steal' those ads. It's fine to blatantly copy someone else's ad (the police won't come knocking on your door), although if you do it to a competitor that's kind of silly and will just lead to places you don't want to go.

4. Take the time to look at ads in competitive markets such as London, New York, Sydney and San Francisco. To keep profitability in these cities is tough. By copying them, you get an idea as to what works and save some time and money

to boot. But rather than just copying, look at their ads – do they use action verbs? How many words are they using? Break the ads down to really understand them.

<u>5. Test an ad for long enough to make sure it's successful.</u> You need to make sure the data is statistically significant – if you stop running an ad after 100 impressions that's just nowhere near enough to give you a good idea of whether it works or not, yet I see operators doing this time and time again.

<u>6. Try putting the pricing in your ads for each tour.</u> There's a good chance you'll notice increased click-throughs – the price calls attention.

<u>7. Use Capitals in Each Word Like This.</u> Otherwise known as Title Case. It's a habit that I got into after using Adwords and seeing that it made a difference.

<u>8. Use numbers & symbols # $ % where possible.</u> Google is sensitive to people jamming symbols into their ads, which means you can't do this: ***!!!CLICKHERE!!!*** However, the appropriate use of the occasional symbol can spike your CTR. In fact, that's half the reason why putting the price in your ad will help you get more clicks – it breaks your ad up visually.

<u>9. Be ready for Google to extend the headline of your ad.</u> In certain cases, Google will attach the 'description line 1' of your ad to your headline, which makes the headline a lot longer. To make this work for you, use a punctuation mark at the end of your description line 1 – Google will take this as a cue to do the headline extension.

<u>10. Use Ad Extensions to blow up your CTR.</u> These things

are gold and Adwords experts have been excitedly sharing the results with me during our conversations (let me tell you, they are seriously impressive.) It gives you the opportunity to include additional data with your ad, such as putting 4 extra links beneath it and it works to draw the attention of the user. There will come a time when these tricks become less effective as users grow accustomed to them, but while the going is hot you should be making the best use of these opportunities.

**11. Use Location Extensions.** If the location of your office is relevant to your clients, add a location extension. This is where Google shows your address and phone number just beneath the ad. It will draw visual attention to your ad and hence, more clicks.

**12. Be vigilant with negative keywords.** Negative keywords are where you tell Google which keywords you don't want to show ads for. Be vigilant to regularly stomp out any keywords which hurt you. I was part of a team that helped save $500,000 a year for a company just by increasing scrutiny on negative keywords.

For example, you might offer Chicago Day Tours that don't visit pizza shops. If someone searches for Chicago Day Tours Pizza then you really don't want to be showing up, because the searcher has a specific intent and you don't match it.

**13. Use different match types.** Test a mix of broad match, exact match and phrase match keywords. I recommend as much use of exact match/phrase match as possible to drill down on user intent. When it comes to broad match – where your ads are shown for searches vaguely related to your business - Google can be very... 'creative'... in their understanding of your campaign, and you'll find your ads being shown for searches that have nothing to do with you at all. That being said, you'll probably generate some new ideas at least.

14. Write descriptive display URLs. Adwords allows you to display a different URL to the one you're sending the visitor to – make it super descriptive and make sure to match the keyword that you're going for.

15. Use a Call-to-Action – let your visitor know the exact action you want them to take. For whatever reason, while we're browsing the internet in our 'auto robot' mode, we're more likely to respond to simple commands. "Book Today!" "Book Your Tour Now" and such are good enough call to actions.

16. Use Dynamic Keyword Insertion – this is where Google automatically inserts the keyword that the user is searching for into the ad. It won't be a surprise to you that when a user sees and ad matching EXACTLY what they just searched for, that there's a good chance they will click it. Be careful with this though – you might end up with a high CTR but low conversions on your landing page when people arrive at a different page to what they were expecting.

17. Most importantly, improve your ad copy. Try and match your language to way that your actual visitors talk about the tours. What sorts of things get them excited? (For example, I can tell you that visitors to Australia are OBSESSED with seeing kangaroos and koalas. It's truly amazing.) Test writing to emotion, the base of human drive – hopes, fears, excitement.

## Adwords – The Final Focus: Raising Your Cost Per Click (CPC)

The goal of nearly all small businesses on Adwords is to lower their Cost Per Click – that is, the amount of money that they're paying for click. This is not the right way to go and if you have this mentality, you have it all wrong!

The key question is this: "How can I increase CPCs and remain profitable?"

Think about it: if you're able to increase the amount of money you're paying per click, this means something is going very well in your business because you have a profitable campaign that is delivering results. If you can bid yourself all the way to number one and still maintain profits, your business is now more or less a money printing machine.

If you're raising your CPC it most likely means that you have a high CTR and a highly-optimized website that is converting. This is why increasing CPC is the ultimate goal.

# Bing, Yahoo And Other Paid Advertising Platforms Will Often Beat Google

Inside the United States, Bing and Yahoo control nearly 30% of searches yet have a far lower proportion of advertisers than Google. That's an untapped opportunity right there and you need to make use of it.

In fact, if you're in the US and currently running a Pay Per Click campaign with an agency through Google and not Bing and Yahoo, there's a good chance you should sack your agency RIGHT now. It's like a baker not adding yeast to their bread or a surgeon forgetting to wash their hands before surgery. You have to be completely incompetent not to do it.

The only exception to this is where thorough investigations and/or tests are conducted which convincingly show that Yahoo/Bing is not an option for you.

## ADVERTISE IN OTHER COUNTRIES AND LANGUAGES

In other English-speaking countries (ie. outside of the USA), Google dominates so much that looking at Bing/Yahoo is almost worthless (unless you have a significant budget.)

If you market to non-English speakers, there's a few search engines which are not Google which are killing it. Yandex in Russia, Baidu in China, Yahoo in Japan (yeh, Yahoo, believe it or not) and Naver in South Korea are the top dogs in their towns.

Besides, advertising in other languages on Google tends to be a lot cheaper per click because of reduced competition. Also, advertising in English to other countries also tends to be very cheap.

Let's take the example of a tour operator in Ecuador. Advertising to people running searches in Latin America is very cheap despite that many of those searches are from people traveling through the area. This means that there's the potential for some great profit margins on your ads.

# PART 8

# TURNING YOUR WEBSITE INTO A SALES MACHINE

What's the point of spending a mountain of money on beautiful vehicles, lovely videos and great marketing if you haven't nailed your website?

Less than 10% of tour operators have a website that's built even mostly correctly. I still haven't found a tour operator website that has nailed all the points below and I've looked at many hundreds of them.

So, while you may well be comfortable with your website, sit up: you shouldn't be, and you're leaving money on the table. Your website can always get better. We're continuously trying to improve the websites of our clients to make them faster, easier to use and more friendly to Google. There's so many ways to improve!

By implementing as much of the advice as possible from the following pages, you should see a lift in sales.

The website sales machine section is divided into 4 parts:

Section A – Getting Images Right

Section B – Writing to Sell

Section C – Designing to Sell

Section D – Converting the Sale

# THE WEBSITE SALES MACHINE

## SECTION A: PHOTOGRAPHY

Great Photos Make a Huge Difference

Up with video and words, photography is one of the top 3 factors for crushing big sales through your site. That being said, if you just put a bunch of pretty photos up on your site what do you think will happen? Not much.

Photos need to serve the business goal, which is to convince more people to book. This means that photos should never get in the way of having a prominent headline on your site, for example.

Like video, which needs to be one of the most prominent things on your site and BIG (not tucked away in the corner like a naughty dog), photography is a major make or break for any website.

Photography doesn't cost much and will deliver you major returns.

1. Avoid stock photography that feels like stock photography. The key is for photos to feel real and genuine.

Ski companies make this mistake all the time, choosing to use random pro photos of some guy skiing down some hill.

For every photo, ask yourself: How does this help you sell YOUR tour? That's the key here.

2. The ideal photo has two heroes: The destination on a

beautiful day and the tour in action. It helps create the feeling of 'I want to do that!' that has people clicking on the 'book now' button. It comes down to the deep-seated 'fear of missing out' that all of us feel. Have you ever seen photos of friends enjoying themselves on a spectacular day and felt a sudden longing to be there? That is what you want in your photos.

3. Upload lots and lots of photos. It's difficult to have too many photos but it is easy to have too few. You have effectively unlimited room at the bottom of your tour descriptions – add a few photos.

4. Encourage guests to send in their photos. From there you can display the good ones on your site.

5. Get a social stream happening of your photos and be uploading constantly. Make it a habit. It shows people that your company is active and popular, two of the biggest factors when it comes to successfully persuading people to take YOUR tour and not one of the many others.

6. Take photos in the early morning or late afternoon when sunlight has its magical golden quality. Some professional photographers are completely and weirdly unaware of this fact (or pretend to be unaware so they can schedule their day more easily), so make sure you insist.

7. Less posing, more fun. Awkward poses are the way photos are done in society but you'll capture more attention with photos of people in the middle of having a blast.

8. No gray clouds. It's surprising how big a difference clouds can make to a photo. I've totally changed the feel of a site just by removing a photo that had a lot of dark

clouds! Try it - you can just feel the difference from photos taken on a beautiful day.

9. Use the rule of thirds. This is a basic rule of photography which says that you shouldn't put anything in the center of a photo (unless you're doing a head-shot). When we have no photo experience we tend to put the horizon in the middle of a photo. Either put the horizon one third from the top or one third from the bottom of a photo. When photographing people, put them one third of the way in from the left or right side. Try it – you'll notice a big difference.

## Hire A College Student Or Someone From A Local Directory Such As Craigslist To Take Your Photos

Photographers will scoff at this next statement, but getting great photos does tend to be much easier than video. Modern-day cameras are so good that they'll do most of the heavy lifting for you.

That being said, you do need someone who considers themselves to be a photographer – even if they're just part time - and has a portfolio. Portfolios matter because someone who has spent the last 10 years doing head shots is generally not in the right head space (pardon the pun) to take photos for your business. The key is to get someone who understands that the photos are to showcase the product that you're trying to sell and NOT for the purposes of winning art competitions.

By hiring someone who is early in their career, you could help them build their portfolio and obviously, you can save a bit of money.

## Get Past Guests To Send In Their Photos

Don't want to carry a camera around? Not sure how to take great photos?

You can take a different route and ask your guests for their permission to use their photos on your site. No doubt you'll have noticed that some of the people who come on your tours are lugging around state of the art cameras with gigantic lenses. Many of these people will be more than happy to pass across their photos.

There's a million ways you can ask them or arrange this, just be careful to make sure that everyone understands that there's no payment involved.

If they're someone who does photography professionally, however, you should expect to pay them.

# THE WEBSITE SALES MACHINE

## SECTION B: USING THE RIGHT WORDS TO WIN A SALE

Surprising Fact: did you know that just by rearranging and changing the words on your site, it's possible for sales to go up by 25%... overnight? If you want to sell people, they need to be convinced and words are the key foundation block for you to build towards this.

Coming right up I've got a few basic tricks to help you nail the foundational details on your own. You'll see for yourself just how much impact words can have, implement some of it yourself and from there go and hire someone to help you extract the most sales possible.

We all know that a smooth talker can have a pretty girl enraptured or that a buffoon has the ability to turn off anyone they meet. There's no weapon mightier than the pen! It's about understanding what people are looking for and worrying about. Then all you have to do is tick their boxes!

## WOULD A SAMURAI CHOOSE YOUR WEBSITE AS THEIR SWORD?

Your website is a shiny sword or a rusty dagger.

How many times have you heard someone justify a movie selection by saying 'it has great reviews'? As humans we look for ways to justify our decision to others in case things don't work out.

When people make their bookings, they don't do it alone. Someone will pick a tour as their favorite and then make the case to their friends or partner to go with you.

Is your website going to help them make that case or get in their way? Is it full of great information and does it answer all the potential questions that someone might have?

Think about it – the winner in your market will often be the person who has the best weapon that helps people make the most convincing arguments to their peers. It's your job to make sure your website gives them the best evidence possible – great photos, video, testimonials, beautiful design, guarantee, and more.

Give your potential guest a nice, big list of arguments that they can use as their armor-piercing weapon. Your website can either be their Exhibit A to make their case or it can be the reason that the group chooses another operator that did a better job than you.

## SET SALES ON FIRE WITH THESE BASIC RULES FOR WEBSITE COPY

Remember why you're writing. Forget everything you learned in school and get back to the PURPOSE of words. We write to communicate, not to impress our English teacher.

Perfect English is not the aim. Grammar matters right up to the point where it interferes with the effectiveness of your communication, and then it doesn't matter one bit. You may have noticed throughout this book that I throw out the rules of the English language where it suits me because I want to write just like I speak. This requires breaking the strait-jackets imposed on us all by our 5th-grade English teachers (who, with respect, have never had to test their words in the hot furnace of a competitive marketplace.)

Here's some basic copywriting tips before we get into the meaty stuff:

1. Have fun. Be interesting. Show your personality.

2. Meaningless adjectives must die – especially where the adjective is bland and generic. Wonderful, amazing, beautiful, fantastic, and best are all words that lose their effect quickly. Of course your tour goes to a beautiful place. Of course you think you have great customer service or the best tour. Of course you're going to say that! Yawn. Give me something interesting!

3. Drop "we" "me" "I" "our" and "us" and change it to "you" and "your." Talk directly to the person you are

writing to. You'll notice that in this book that I use the word "you" incessantly because I want to communicate with you. Write as if you're writing just to one person. Think of your typical favorite client even. If you were to write a message directly to them on Facebook or by email, how would you talk to them? Write like this.

4. Be direct. Change "you will see the bridge with us" to "see the bridge with us." Get them to feel it.

5. Read it out loud. Many writing mistakes can be picked up just by reading your words back to yourself.

6. Pass it to someone else to read. What do they think is boring? Unconvincing? Pointless? Lacking in formation?

7. Put your most important information first. People won't give you the time of day if you're wasting words at the top of a page. Too much work, they'll think.

8. Write for scanners. Basically no one sits down and reads entire web pages any more, unless they are SUPER fascinating. That doesn't mean you need to write less words, however. It just means that you need to structure your content in a different way.

9. Remember that the home page is often not the first page someone will see, A lot of visitors to your site will arrive at a different page, so each one needs to be written in such a way that a first time visitor gets what is going on.

10. Use the simple alternative for words. A large percentage of visitors to your website are not highly educated or don't speak English as a first language.

## THIS TRICK WILL HAVE PEOPLE BEGGING TO BOOK WITH YOU

There's a fantastic trick which you can use in writing to make people super keen to book with you. Curious to find out what it is?

Of course you would like to know, and that is the trick! I'm talking about curiosity.

Compare these two sentences:

"We will visit the Jordan Tower, which has 88 stories and offers wonderful views of the entire city." ? This is boring and generic.

"Come with us to the spectacular top of 88 story Jordan Tower - the tallest in Asia! Learn the ingenious methods used by its engineers to conquer its challenges and why they chose to keep heat out of the restaurant with 100% pure gold leaf paint." ? Not perfect, but much better.

It's not just about selling the destination, it's also about selling how your company has the exclusive knowledge to make it doubly interesting.

Think of the interesting facts that you share on your trip and then share half of it, leaving your website visitor to wonder what the rest is!

## GIVE THEM THE FEAR OF MISSING OUT

If you've ever been to Booking.com – the hotel booking website – you'll know what it's like to have fear of missing out. This fear is one of the prime human drivers – we just can't handle having an opportunity taken away from us.

Booking.com does this brilliantly. When you're looking at a hotel they might have a notice saying something like "hurry! Only 2 rooms left!" In that moment, you go from being a casual browser to someone who has to decide right now.

(For the cynics, Booking.com is telling the truth here – otherwise they'd get dragged into a world of pain by the FTC, who are tough on this stuff.)

Just by putting a notice such as "Hurry - most tours sell out" next to your booking button or pricing, you'll create urgency.

If you have a mechanism on your site which shows exactly how many spots are left for that day, even better. You don't need a $200/hr programmer to whip this up for you, either. Many of the tour booking software options available around the place allow you the option.

Another idea worth trying out is another trick from Booking.com where they say "2 people are looking at this hotel right now." It really moves you into action and forces you to decide (at least for me!).

# Your About Page Will Be One Of The Top 3 Visited Pages – Make Use Of This Valuable Real Estate

When was the last time you looked at your About Page? A while ago, I'd bet. It's perfectly natural to think that this page lacks in importance but take a look at your statistics. You'll find that it's one of the most visited on your site. This means it COULD make the crucial difference in winning that booking.

The key here is to create a personal connection with the visitor to your site. If they like you, they will want to go with you!

Some tips:

a) Name the page "Our Guides" or anything less bland than "About."

b) Share your personal story but in first person. Third person is impersonal by design, which worries me. You should avoid it where possible.

c) Make the headline of the page interesting. It could a quote from your personal story but it needs to be a hook to get things going.

d) Showcase your team properly, if you have one.

e) Use photos of your team and yourself in the wild. Awkward smiles in front of a wall as they are for businesses that are having way less fun than you!

# THE B.E.T.T.E.R METHOD FOR WRITING TOUR DESCRIPTIONS

How would you propose marriage to someone? Think for a second. I wouldn't do it in my gym clothes, that's for sure. I also wouldn't do it while in the supermarket looking for vegetables.

If you want to propose marriage to someone, you will dress up nice, take your loved one to a beautiful location and do it there. The key here is that you take your time and do it right.

Your tour description is THE moment where you propose marriage to your potential customer – a marriage of their money and your wallet! It is when you set yourself apart and make them rush to choose YOU and no one else. In the SEO section of this book, I talked about using keywords in your descriptions and writing rich copy. Let's dive in a little deeper.

Writing out a basic description is not enough. Unless you are in the middle of nowhere, you have competition. Even if you are the only person offering your specific tour, they will always have other options. You need to write with detail and follow the principle of 'more is more'. Less is more may apply to some things but it most DEFINITELY does not apply to tour descriptions. You need to almost overwhelm people with information.

Follow the 'BETTER' Method to write a great description and you will be WAY ahead of the pack.

Basic Breakdown – Start out your summary with a basic breakdown and bullet points of the major attractions you are going to including the price, starting point and other basic details.

Exhibit the Experience – Lay out in great detail the tour while keeping the curiosity factor. Use sub-headlines and short paragraphs to break up the information and include photos so people can see what they are getting.

Short and sweet will NOT help you sell. It's a myth. People are risking their holiday experience with you. Go into detail.

Tick Their Boxes – What do people need to know? Do you cater for disabled people? Children? Are meals included? What do they need to bring? Are admission fees included? Have you listed literally every single place you go to? Who knows what your potential guest has in mind! Get it all out on your site.

Testimonials – Include testimonials you have received for that specific tour. Make sure the testimonials reference specific highlights of your tour, rather than the generic 'we loved it!' type of testimonials that one sees around. Include photos (or videos) where possible.

Expertise – In your description, demonstrate your specific expertise that makes the tour magic. How your local knowledge gives YOU insider secrets and history that they could never tap into anywhere else.

Reservation – At the bottom of your description, have a call to action – a gigantic button, a contact form, a calendar of availability - to guide people to book. Whatever it is, the end of your description should flow into the exact action you want your website visitor to take.

# The Mistake That Too Many Custom Tour Providers Make – Not Providing Example Itineraries

A basic principle of marketing anything is that you shouldn't make people work to figure out what you're offering. This is a mistake that too many custom tour providers are making.

What I'm saying is this: if you do custom tours, there's no law against providing sample itineraries!

Sample itineraries help people understand what it is you actually do. Create different itineraries according to the different types of inquiries that you receive.

For example, winery tour operators might create a sample Boutique Winery Tour for those who love visiting tiny wineries and want to chat with the owner. Other visitors want to check out the wineries of the brands they already know and love – call it The Greatest Hits Winery Tour.

Forcing people to use their own imagination to create a tour of a place they most likely have never even visited before is a quick way to go out of business. You're putting the onus on your guest to do the work. This is crazy.

Show your expertise up front by showing your visitor the kind of experience they could have with you.

I'd recommend placing at least 4-5 example itineraries, but don't call them 'example' itineraries – make it look like a tour that they can easily book - emphasizing that the entire experience is customizable. Alongside your itineraries on the home page, have a specific section for custom tours so those people who are genuinely looking for customized experiences can have it.

Try it: you'll see that many of your inquiries and bookings will come in for your pre-created tours.

## SHOW THAT YOU'RE THE BOSS SOCKS

You need to exploit every potential advantage.

One way to do this is to show exactly why you (or your team) are the one to make someone's holiday dreams come true. This stuff needs to be right up the top so that even blind Freddy (or blind Jenny) couldn't miss it.

How you can incorporate this information into your site?

1. How many years experience do you or your team have in delivering tours?
2. How long has your business been open?
3. How many successful tours have you run?
4. What is your industry experience? For example, you may not have been running tours for long but you could be a renowned expert in your field.
5. What qualifications do you have?
6. What is your environmental impact?
7. What are your industry association endorsements and memberships?
8. What kind of equipment do you use? How new is it? Does it have safety ratings?
9. What insurance do you have?
10. What safety certifications do you have? What's your safety record?

11. What social proof do you have? Which leads to our next tip...

## SOCIAL PROOF: WHAT IT IS AND WHY YOU NEED TO EXPLOIT IT TO THE MAX

Have you ever walked past an empty restaurant and then straight into a full one despite not knowing anything about EITHER restaurant... just because of safety in numbers?

Welcome to social proof – where people make a decision to buy something based on its popularity.

In Robert Cialdini's excellent book "Influence: The Psychology of Persuasion", the author explains just how powerful an influence it can be to see a crowd choose something. Take the example of canned laughter on TV shows – everyone says they hate it, but observation shows that people laugh more and show more satisfaction with television shows that use it.

You'd remember the extreme pressure to conform in high school. This instinct stays with us right to the grave even if it's a little less obvious at times.

Social proof shows that you are credible, popular and that other people are having great experiences with you. This has a powerful effect on how people perceive your business. This is the underlying principle as to why businesses with boatloads of great TripAdvisor reviews will generate more bookings.

A few examples of social proof:

*Sell More Tours*

1. Photos of people having fun on your tour.
2. News-media or blog mentions.
3. Industry association memberships (as mentioned before).
4. TripAdvisor excellence badges
5. To a lesser extent, embedding your Facebook widget can help if it has a lot of likes.
6. Major awards.
7. The most important: legitimate testimonials. Which leads to the next chapter.

# How To Win At The Game Of Testimonials

Right now, you're aware of the importance of testimonials. It just so happens that there's more to it than just putting up a testimonials page and copy-pasting in the emails you receive.

Testimonials suffer from credibility issues. So many websites have used fake testimonials that anything you use needs to feel as real as possible to ward off cynicism.

How to win the game of testimonials:

1. Use reviews posted on other sites. This is the quickest way to ensure that a review appears legitimate and not faked. Quote the review and link to the source of the review.

2. Video testimonials can open a world of difference. You can whip out a camera during a trip with a happy guest and ask them what they think. (If must give credit to Tim Warren from Travel Business Success for that tip.)

3. Make sure any testimonials you receive are as specific as possible in terms of what made the guest so happy to travel with you.

4. Real names and real photos go a long way. Quoting just the initials of someone looks fake. But won't people object to having their names on your site?

Some people are worried about having their name on the internet. That's fine – you don't HAVE to include their testimonial on your site. That simple.

5. When presenting the testimonial on your site, take the best quote available from the testimonial and make it a 'headline' of it. You put this at the top of the testimonial so people are drawn into reading the entire thing.

6. Make the testimonials PROMINENT. Great testimonials will be one of your super-power sales weapons. Sadly, too many tour operators (or their silly web designers, let's be honest here) hide their testimonials away. Bring them into the light and let them shine brighter than Jim Carrey's teeth.

7. If you get a great testimonial, share it on social media. You don't need to spam your social media with testimonials but once or twice a month does the trick. If people like your business, they will be happy for you and you'll be reinforced as a great business in their mind.

8. Quote your testimonials in all printed materials such as brochures or posters.

9. Quote your testimonials in your profile description on TripAdvisor. Quote one sentence each from two different testimonials and you'll be fine.

# The Secret Gold Mine In The Questions You Get Asked

Every time someone sends you a question, do you see it as a hassle or as gold-plated FREE market research?

Do you have questions that are coming up repeatedly? Then, how clearly are those questions answered on your website? If you're answering the same questions over and over, this is clearly an issue!

Put a frequently asked questions section at the bottom of every tour description, riiiiight at the end, for those people who are still scrolling and don't have all of their concerns addressed.

Copywriting guru Joanna Wiebe from CopyHackers.com) has a favorite tactic for writing on clients' sites: talk to the actual customers and then only use those words in the copy.

It's a strategy that's so stupidly clever that few of us are even smart enough to have even thought of it! We have our own way of explaining things or describing things but the way to really connect with our guests is to use the words they would use.

Given you're a tour operator this is kind of simple. You spend all day long talking with your guests, so you know exactly how they talk.

Ask yourself: "have I ever heard a customer use these words? This terminology?" If the answer is no then have a good hard think about how much you want to include those words or consider putting an explanation instead.

## ADDRESS THE FUDS (FEARS, UNCERTAINTIES AND DOUBTS) OF YOUR PROSPECTS

Committing to spend money on your tour is a significant risk for the person who does it. They've spent a lot time dreaming of their holiday and are now trusting it to you. Into your hands.

You're going to need their trust. Showing your expertise and social proof contributes to this but we need to go further.

What do you find people are worried about before booking your tour? You'll often find that people begin to worry about factors that pop up in negative TripAdvisor reviews – both of your business and similar businesses. In positive reviews you'll see people saying things like "we were worried there'd be too many people to enjoy it, but it was perfect." Take note of these worries.

When you book a tour, you're not just thinking of you. You've also got in mind the people coming with you. This causes people to be especially cautious - if you book for yourself and it doesn't work, fine, but if you book for someone else and it doesn't work... then they'll blame you.

Take all the Fears, Uncertainties and Doubts people have and address them in the words on your website and you'll go a long way to winning more sales.

If your website deals perfectly with FUDs it helps people can justify their decision to book with you if something goes wrong. Don't underestimate the power of this. Some tour operators have implemented JUST this change to their site and gone from nearly broke to having a successful business.

The person advocating to book with you will make use of the FUD information you have on your site to help sell their friends.

What are people worried about when they get in touch with you? Are they worried about the weather? Are they worried that they might not see a dolphin? Do what you can to try and create that safety blanket in which they feel warm, cozy and safe with you.

# OFFER A GREAT GUARANTEE TO OVERCOME FEARS, UNCERTAINTIES AND DOUBTS

One of the biggest jobs of selling on a website is to convince people to take the risk of giving you money without ever having met you.

Buying something without having ever seen it is a genuine, big risk. You may know your tour is fantastic but your potential guest won't be so sure. In fact, most of the points of this book are all about overcoming the sense of risk that someone feels – great photos, great testimonials... the whole kit and kaboodle is all about making people feel safe booking with you, a complete stranger.

One of the most powerful ways to enhance the risk-free nature of your service is to offer a convincing guarantee. 'Happiness guaranteed or your money back' is fairly standard but it's possible to go further.

Tourism operators who take people to see animals often will say things like 'see 5 dolphins or receive a ticket to come back, free!' That kind of guarantee can be powerful – I should know because 10 years ago, I chose one dolphin tour company over another specifically because of that guarantee and still remember it.

What kind of guarantee could you offer?

Probably the biggest barrier for small businesses owners when they offer a guarantee is a feeling of risk – what would happen if people take advantage of it? The fact that you feel a fear of offering a guarantee should be the perfect demonstration of WHY you should be offering a guarantee – finally you're understanding how your potential customer feels. Do you want them to feel that small nagging doubt or do YOU want to feel it? Do you really want to saddle that emotion onto their shoulders?

People very rarely will take you up on your guarantee. If people are regularly asking for their money back, it's a clear sign that you have a genuinely terrible product and need to fix it which is a harsh way to receive that message but better to receive the message rather than stick your head in the sand.

# THE WEBSITE SALES MACHINE

# SECTION C: DESIGN THAT SELLS

Some websites convert 1.5% of their visitors into sales. Others convert 2.5%. Have you ever wondered what you can do to increase that percentage? Think about it: it could be THE most important percentage in your business.

Just by increasing your conversion rate from 2% to 2.2% you'll increase your revenues by 10%. All this just by converting a TINY 0.2% of extra visitors to sales.

Think about the power of this. Do you think there could possibly be some changes you make to your site that might convert an extra 0.2% of visitors to sales? You're just about to learn secrets that even most web designers aren't aware of.

Many of the following tips will seem almost obvious, but try to remember the last time you saw a tour operator website that nailed all these factors (or even half of them).

You spend so much time looking at your own website that you can't be a good judge of it. People coming to it for the first time are having a completely different experience to you! They don't know your product offering and are lost when they arrive at the home page of your site.

The distracted nature of the majority of internet browsing means that your website needs to accommodate for this.

Our goal is to remove even the tiniest obstacles which cause people to give up. It needs to be super easy to use and more so than you would think.

I your website was launched before 2011, it doesn't matter how nice it looks, you need a new one. The majority of current web technology has been developed during or after 2011. In fact, most websites built in 2011 or later are also generally built incorrectly as web designers struggle to get with the times. C'est la vie.

User experience is everything. Remember the section about SEO earlier in this book? I explained that having a good user experience has become a plank in your Google ranking. Neglect it to your peril.

According to a survey released by marketing software maker HubSpot, for 76% of users the most important factor in a website is that "the website makes it easy to find what I want." In the coming pages of the book, I'll share with you the lessons I've learned in terms of making sure a website is easy to use for anyone who visits your website.

Before we start on this process though, there's one thing you need to understand: without the proper investment of time and money, you're drastically lowering your chances of real success – that's why we call it an investment!

## As Obvious As A Brick In The Face

I call it the 'Drunk Old Guy Principle'. Here it is: When an 80 year old drunk Italian who has bad eyesight and struggles a little with English visits your site, does he understand what you do and what he needs to do next?

And I don't just refer to the home page. Every. Single. Page. needs to have a glaringly obvious purpose.

The headline of your site should be readable from several yards away from your computer. That's the kind of obvious I'm talking about.

Internet users in browsing mode more or less have their brains switched off. There's a good chance they're watching television at the same time or juggling some other activity such as managing children or five Facebook conversations.

A huge, descriptive headline along with a great photo and an obvious place to click is what combats this and grabs their focus. I've seen the proof of this countless times in the statistics of clients over the years, such that this should be the first change you make to your site.

Take your visitor by the hand and guide them. Every single page on the site needs to have an obvious next step that you want the guest to take. This is something very few tour operator websites do.

Most home pages have a photo or two, some awards, a bit of text and that's it - the guest is expected to take the initiative to figure out what to do next.

In addition, your tour listings and descriptions need to have a prominent call to action – don't just expect that people will automatically go looking for your bookings and inquiries page, because many simply won't.

## Your Website Needs To Run Faster Than Usain Bolt And Marion Jones' Love Child... Souped Up On Steroids!

Here's a totally unsurprising fact: people like using faster websites.

Here's the totally unsurprising consequence of that fact: faster websites make more sales.

Studies by companies such as Google, Yahoo and Amazon have all shown that website speed makes a non-trivial difference to their bottom line – in fact, many studies report that for every 1 second of delay in the first few seconds, a website will lose about 7% of sales.

7%. That's a LOT of sales to lose for a one second delay.

To test the performance of your own site, run a search for "Google Pagespeed Insights." If your site gets less than 80% across any of the categories, your website needs help! (In my own testing, I've never seen a website get more than 90% across all three.)

If a new website isn't a possibility, have a chat with your web designer about what they can do to clean that score up.

It's Google's very own tool, which means you're getting a sneak-peak insight into how they view your own website. Google has publicly stated that website speed affects how much you pay per click on Adwords and your search engine rankings. Have a think about that.

# Track Which Marketing Sources Are Performing Best With Google Analytics

Most tour operators in today's age have Google Analytics installed on their site. It's a great little piece of software but the information will often not help you all that much if you do not tell it what the goal of your website is. Google Analytics can not read your mind (yet), so we need to tell it what we want from our site. This way, it knows what we consider to be a success – and then it can report on this.

For example, when people book a tour with you they'll often be taken to a "Thank-you For Your Booking" Page. There's only one way for them to get to that page – they've booked something with you. As such, the goal is to get people to that page.

Once Google Analytics knows this, it can then track all visitors who arrive to your booking confirmation page and then mark them as a success. From there, you'll be able to see exactly which visitor sources are delivering your customers. This is SUPER-DUPER-POWERFUL data.

From now on you'll be able to see which of your traffic sources are kicking butt and which are failing. A common complaint of those using Google Adwords is that they can't tell if it's working or not. No longer!

Added to this, Google now offers something called Assisted Conversion Tracking. If someone comes in through one traffic source and then returns to buy from another, you'll be able to see this in Analytics. Now you can see the actual sources of your customers! It could be the case that Google Adwords is working a lot better for you than you thought it was.

As to the actual process to set up Goals, it's hard to describe in a book but your web consultant should be able to help you set them up in a jiffy – we do it for all our customers for when their websites go live and you'll find that many other companies do the same. Alternately, there's tutorials online including one at tourismeschool.com and we'll be posting videos at some point up to our website with instructions – visit tourismtiger.com/videos.

# The Number One Goal Of Your Home Page Is Not What You Think It Is

Have you ever stopped to consider what the number one goal of your home page is?

All that design, all those photos, all that text: to what end? Most home pages have no obvious idea as to what they want the visitor to do next. If you have a page about a specific tour, for example, it's easy to write content for that and direct people towards that goal. But your home page? Hmm.

Well, here's your answer: <u>The goal of a home page is to convince a visitor to click somewhere.</u>

That's it. That's all you need to aim for. Give them at least one big shiny thing to click on, right in the center of the screen.

That first click is crucial. It's the first step to getting someone to engage with your website, the place from which we can send them down the rabbit hole. By doing this we decrease the bounce rate of your site and get people to hang around for longer, eventually increasing sales.

# Put Your Phone Number and At Least One Credibility Statement In Your Site's Header

This is becoming less and less important unless your business relies on telephone inquiries.

Back in the day when people were much more suspicious of the internet, you could increase sales just by including a phone number on your site to show you had a legitimate business.

While it's now less important, that doesn't mean it shouldn't be done.

Add some sort of credibility statement to your website's header in addition to your phone number.

"1,432 clients since 1996"

"#1 on TripAdvisor for 2013"

and so on and so forth.

## ADD A LIVE CHAT WIDGET TO YOUR SITE

You've probably seen these around: live chat widgets where you can chat to a website operator (or at the least, a customer service person) are becoming de rigeur on many sites.

Most of them are executed poorly as most live chat widgets sit passively in the background hoping.

It's better for a chat tool to automatically pop up and try to engage a chat – if you can get a guest involved in a chat, you astronomically increase your chances of getting a booking as you have a chance to create a memorable personal connection with them which is the key. People assume these are just robots – so if you say "I'm actually here" to your visitor, this helps.

Recommended Tools:

1. SnapEngage.com

2. ClickDesk.com

3. ZOPim.com

I've had rather uncomfortable live chat experiences where the operator keeps on trying to push me into having a phone call. While the idea to engage is correct, the technique is not.

Rather than just sit and answer their questions, you can also ask questions of them and engage them in conversation. You can also do things during the chat session such as offer them a free ebook or even a discount code for the trip they are enquiring about. Have a think about what exact things you can do to create a human-level connection with the person you are talking to.

Additionally, make sure to include your name and photo in the chat widget so your website visitor can get a good idea of who they are talking to.

If you have office staff who man the phone and keep your operation humming, it's easy to get one of them to sit on live chat each day as well. You won't get a huge amount of people trying to engage with you but it's worth having it available. As a website visitor, I love using live chat widgets to ask questions – it's much easier than sending an email. Just make sure that you or the staff member using it uses it. Many people forget to sign in each day which means your widget just sits there offline, looking silly.

# How To Reduce Your Bounce Rate

In your Google Analytics account, you'll notice that your bounce rate is displayed prominently. The term bounce rate refers to those people who hit your website and leave without taking any further action.

It's important to note that Google does NOT use the bounce rate you see in Analytics as a way to determine rankings. For their own rankings, they use a different idea called the 'long click'. Google can see when someone clicks on a search engine result to go to your website. From there it's not difficult to then measure how many people come back to Google by clicking the back button. Google's measure of a quality outcome is for people to click on a website in their search results and never come back.

The bounce rate measure you see in Google Analytics includes other things besides, such as people closing their browser when they hit your site. This exact statistic doesn't impact on your search results but it clearly affects your sales, so we need to reduce it.

To reduce our bounce rate, we have one singular goal: to get someone to click somewhere. This needs to be done on navigation pages (such as the home page) as this is where the majority of your visitors will arrive. It's a simple exercise: all you need to do is give people something to click on. That's it!

What tends to work well is either a gigantic button in the center of the screen, or tiles with photos of each tour that drive the click. I learned this when I worked for one of Australia's largest digital marketing agencies. My job was to manage the online marketing campaigns of around 60 websites, a large chunk of them in the tourism space.

One day I noticed that one of the websites in our care had an extraordinarily low bounce rate (it was around 20-25%). Being so low, I decided to take the time to figure out why and it turned out that the reason was the use of tiles in the navigation (tiles are basically clickable thumbnails with photos and some text description.)

Note: if you have a bounce rate of below 10% this most likely means you have the Google Analytics code installed on your website twice, which mucks with the code. Every website I have ever seen with a bounce rate below 10% was suffering from this issue.

# IT NEEDS TO BE EASIER TO READ THAN YOU THINK

Mobile devices. Small monitors. Difficult light. Bad eyesight. There's many reasons text can often be more difficult to read than you might think.

Speaking for myself, I have some difficulty reading websites with dark backgrounds and will generally do everything I can to avoid them. It's all about making your website a pleasurable place to be.

Some tips:

1. Body text should always be dark text on a light background.

2. Do you have any elderly relatives? Take a look at your website again. Could they read it without problems or would they be squinting up against the monitor? Asking yourself this question is a good basic rule to follow.

3. The text size should be larger than you think and with a decent amount of space between each line.

4. Break the text up into small chunks.

5. Bold anything that's important, such as your key points of difference or the important things in your tour.

# Responsive Design For Mobile Devices: Without It, Your Website Is Most Definitely Obsolete

At the time of writing, most tour operators are getting 45-50% of their visitors from mobile devices and growing. This means that your mobile website is now MORE important than your 'normal' website.

Responsive design makes your website shift size to fit whatever device it is being seen on. It will fit perfectly on an iPhone screen and on a normal desktop computer while being exactly the same website.

You must be able to cater to mobile devices in a modern world. Catering to only one half of your visitors is website insanity. We know this because in a Google survey, "67% of users said they're more likely to purchase a product or service from a site that is mobile-friendly" and "48% of users become frustrated and annoyed when on sites that have been either been poorly optimized or not optimized at all (for mobile)"

Before writing this book I had the good fortune to interview Peep Laja of ConversionXL, one of the world's top experts on improving website conversions. He told me this:

"I've never seen an instance where a website has not increased its sales as a result of changing their design to responsive."

Without responsive design your website is living in the past and making less sales. As a technology, it has replaced mobile websites as the standard for dealing with mobile devices. The reason is simple – companies keep bringing out new devices of all shapes and sizes and mobile websites just cannot keep up. In today's world, there are thousands of different mobile devices and you need to be able to cater to all of them.

Sounds difficult? It doesn't have to be. As you now know, responsive design automatically adjusts itself to all devices. Problem solved!

Add a Tap to Call Button on Mobiles

If your business is the type that takes bookings over phone calls, you can add a tap-to-call button on your responsive website.

Whenever someone visits from a device below a certain screen size – basically, anything smaller than an iPad mini - they will automatically see a button that says 'Tap Here to Call'. This makes it easier – hence more likely – for them to call.

## ATTRACTIVE DESIGN HELPS SALES – BOTH DIRECTLY AND INDIRECTLY

Having an attractive website will help your sales. (There, I said it. Controversial stuff.) While any web designer will tell you that an attractive design will help sales as if it's the be-all end-all, this is just one component of a larger experience.

Attractive designs are like attractive people – for better or for worse, you tend to linger around them. Having said that, a beautiful website is the cherry on top and as such it must serve your business goals and not conflict with them. .

This is an indisputable fact: fairly or not, SOME people will judge you on the design of your website. These people use the quality of a design to measure the quality of a business. Maybe living in a world full of Apple products has taught people to make this association. Either way, it helps to take into an account.

Here are the effects of an attractive site:

1. Increased time on site. When a site is attractive and pleasant to be around, your statistics will show that people linger for longer and as a consequence give you more of a chance to sell them.

2. Increased bookings. As mentioned, a major factor when people are booking on behalf of others is that they need be able to defend their decision. An attractive site is a great weapon for this.

3. **Improved SEO** as people are more willing to link to you. When a website owner links to your site, it reflects on their own credibility so they tend to link to great looking businesses. Moz.com, which is the leading informational site about SEO, has called this the 'no one likes to link to a crummy site' phenomenon.

4. **Increased social sharing** – for the same reason as before, people feel more comfortable sharing things on social media which are likely to reflect well on them.

5. **Improve your chances of industry partnerships**. Once again, this comes back to the 'I may need to defend my choice' phenomenon. When larger companies are looking to select partners, their employees' main priority is to make a defensible decision. If you nail all the steps in this book AND have an attractive design, you'll go far.

# THE WEBSITE SALES MACHINE

## SECTION D: CONVERT THE SALE

They've seen your photos. They've read the great tour descriptions. They've found your website a pleasure to use. Now for the final step: close the sale and get those who are on the fence to book with you now.

## FOLLOW UP FAST

Did you know that the speed at which you reply to an inquiry is more important than what you say? In fact, multiple studies have shown that you can increase conversions of inquiries to sales by several hundred percent just by responding within the first 30 minutes.

On paper, this will seem crazy but when you think about it... it still seems crazy!

When you get a question or request, you're in the running as a potential candidate. There's a good chance you're even the #1 choice. But the longer you leave it, the more the person who contacted you cools off. They're going to keep browsing and might find a company who excites them even more, because of this rock-solid written-in-stone fact:

Emotions fade.

After sending you the message, the excitement begins to disappear. Just one day later they may not really care all that much. They've forgotten how looking at your photos made their heart race or how your testimonials made them feel secure.

There's a reason why the expression 'strike while the iron is hot' is so popular. Make use of this understanding and turn it to your advantage.

Not only this, but by replying quickly you'll establish yourself as someone who is available and dependable in the minds of your potential guest.

## HAVE A FOLLOW-UP SYSTEM

Someone inquires with you. What happens next? While this is MOST important for businesses that handle larger sales, it's important for all businesses.

If you're selling tours of decent value, track inquiries in a spreadsheet or CRM. While this sounds like a drag (and is), you can automate the process in many ways using tools available online, which helps you link your pieces of software together.

People will get distracted by the hustle and bustle of daily life. If you have valuable leads, don't let them walk away without a few nudges...!

If you sell tours of lower value, you can still place them into an automated followup series which requires zero work from you besides the initial setup.

If you have a concrete follow-up system that you will increase the number of sales to these people. I guarantee it.

A Trick To Help You Follow Up Fast

Sitting around all day refreshing your email doesn't sound like much of a good time.

That's why you need to use either SMS Notification or Phone Call Notification for all new leads. We offer this to our customers and there's a good chance your current agency does, too.

Our system converts your email inquiry into an automatic SMS or phone call. The faster you respond, the more likely you are to win the business. Implementing something like this will help you achieve this.

Aim for a 5 Minute Response Time. Why not? You need to respond at some point so you might as well make it snappy. This is something I've struggled with in my own business but we're working on it. Start to grind that time down by measuring those stats and you're on the right path.

Setting this sort of thing up is super affordable – we charge peanuts for it. It's so affordable that I recommend it to literally all tourism businesses, no matter their size.

Track Your Response Time Easily Using Online Tools

You may not be able to aim for a 5 minute turnaround time on customer service emails, but you CAN track your overall response time and begin driving it down.

You can do this using an online help desk tool which -importantly – just looks like email to you client. They think that they're emailing you and you're responding to them, but the actual truth is that you're managing it all on the back-end with a system.

Previously, help desks had an elaborate process of registering yourself on their software, creating a ticket and then waiting for a response. No longer!

The three most popular examples of this new type of tool at time of writing are Groove HQ, HelpScout and SupportBee (I'm a user of HelpScout).

It's like having an email inbox on steroids. Each service listed above has its own advantages but the key one we're looking for is being able to track response time. At any time, you can see your response time and as they say, you can't improve it if you're not measuring it.

One more thing: if you own a larger operation and have dedicated support staff, please don't walk over to their desk right now and dump the 5 minute response time expectation on their shoulders with no warning or preparation. It's unfair to them.

Be deliberate about your processes and make sure you work along-side your staff to create and optimize them. The first step needs to be setting up a system where a new customer service email creates a notification so that you or your team know an email has arrived – as mentioned in the previous tip.

## Answer The Bloody Phone

Some of the bits of advice in this book may seem obvious. "Answer your phone" is a case in point.

"Really? Answer the phone? Great advice, Sherlock," is what you may be thinking. That being said, the only reason any of the points in this book are listed is because I've seen people consistently getting it wrong.

On a holiday in Malaysia in 2013, I decided I wanted to go diving the very next day after a previous plan was canceled by an operator. Looking to salvage my holiday, that afternoon I went to the website of a tour operator and they didn't answer my phone call.

A key thing to remember here is that most international tourists don't have working telephone lines so it won't be easy for them to call you. If they do manage to call you it's going to be on someone else's phone and will most likely cost a pretty dime.

In my desperation, I took a taxi down to their office but being 4pm it had closed for the evening. I tried to call again. No answer. Tried their mobile phone. No answer.

Then, I discovered on their website the cell number of their head dive instructor. She promised to get back to me. 5 hours later, silence. I called again and at 10pm at night I finally had my booking. How many customers has this business lost because of their inability to answer phones and be available?

If you're going to have a phone number on your site, be ready for calls.

## DIAL UP YOUR CONTACT METHODS

Not too long ago, I found a small business that had listed their WhatsApp details where they said "Contact Us!.

Being an avid WhatsApp user, I thought this was pretty cool and decided to contact them using that. Who knows if I would have bothered to get in touch otherwise?

Listing a multitude of contact methods is a great idea but only if you're going to monitor the methods. The business in the example mentioned is a case in point. I sent them a WhatsApp message and they took 2 days to respond.

While things such as Twitter or Facebook can send you email notifications (which can be converted into SMS/Phone Call Notifications as mentioned earlier), services like WhatsApp, Viber and WeChat are just smartphone apps, meaning people will message you at any time of the day or night.

In many cases, having an unusual contact method will spark a smile in someone and help convert them into an inquiry.

Bonus Tip 1: If you're going to go down this path, make sure that you get the same user-name/handle on as many of these services as possible, otherwise you will confuse people.

Bonus Tip 2: If you're going to list these details on a company site, make sure your profile on these details is consistent with what you have listed on the site. When you respond from a personal account with a photo of your children, you may confuse them.

## Make Your Inquiry Form As Difficult To Use As Possible (Or Not)

Let's just say I have a simple question for you: "Do you operate on New Years Day?"

That should be easy for me to ask, right? Why, then, do some operators present me with a booking form that asks me for all sorts of details?

I just want to ask a question! If someone calls you up do you force them to answer 10 questions before you get around to answering them? No, of course not.

If you take bookings via a form, make a booking form and a contact form and for both forms, chop down the form fields to the barest minimum the amount of information needed. For the love of everything good and right, don't make me work to give you money.

I recommend providing your email along with the form. Some people prefer to use forms, other people prefer to email directly. I'm in the latter camp because too many times I have submitted an inquiry to a form and ... nothing. Make sure the email you provide is a clickable link so if they have a native email program, it will open straight away.

# The Booking Button: Bigger Than Godzilla

Get yourself a big 'even blind drunk 80 year old Freddy couldn't miss it' booking button.

Here's a few tips:

1. Make it obvious. The booking button needs to be the most clearly identifiable part of the page. If someone were to take their glasses off, they should be able to still identify the booking button.

2. Use contrasting color. The color of the booking button needs to really stand out. It should be the one time you see that color on that page.

3. Use imperatives such as "Book Now" as opposed to "Bookings and inquiries." People need to be guided through the booking process – our lizard brain is looking for pointers as to what to do next.

4. Use personal pronouns. For example: "Book My Tour " as opposed to "Book a Tour." Interestingly, we used to recommend using "Book Your Tour" but a few tests around the internet have shown that "My" generally beats "Your" as a best practise.

5. Create a sense of urgency and immediacy. For example "Book My Tour Now"

6. Fear of Missing Out. If possible, squeeze a bit of FOMO in there too. That's why my favorite booking button text is something like "Book My Spot Now", "Book My Place

Now" or "Reserve My Place Now." For some reason, the word 'spot' makes it feel like there's just one seat for me and someone could snatch it away, which is why it's my favorite.

7. Make it pop out of the design – it should stick out or not fit into the neat symmetry of the site. Make it so that your brain cannot ignore it and surround that thing with empty space so it has no other visual distractions.

# The Booking Button: Two Additional Tricks To Close People Who Are On The Fence

<u>Trick One: Click Triggers Give Them The Final Nudge</u>

Just near the booking button is an empty space and opportunity.

Click Triggers are little things you put near the booking button to get rid of last minute anxieties. They're reminders of why they should book with you. Joanna Wiebe from CopyHackers.com deserves all the credit for this one.

I'd put two things:

<u>A "Fear of Missing Out" trigger</u>. For example - "Hurry – Tours Book Fast," "Get Your Seat Before They're Gone" or "Numbers Strictly Limited."

<u>A "Confidence"</u> trigger such as a reference to the amount of 5 star reviews you have on TripAdvisor, or your money back guarantee. "100% Satisfaction Guaranteed."

<u>Trick Two: Booking Button Follows Your Guest Down The Screen</u>

Staying with booking buttons for now, did you know it's possible to make it so that the booking button follows your guest down the screen as they scroll?

As an example of how this might be implemented, for the websites my company makes the booking button stays 'sticky' in the top right of the screen. This means that it always sits there as a presence, impossible to ignore. On mobile devices, the booking button is designed to stay at the top of the screen and follow them down.

It won't double your sales or even close to it but it's worthwhile. Success online is all increasing things by 1% here or there to a big overall result.

## "IN GOD WE TRUST... EVERYONE ELSE MUST BRING DATA" - WHY YOUR WEBSITE NEEDS TESTING

Google hires some of the brightest, most intelligent people in the world. Yet even in their hallways, opinions are not allowed: if you think you're right about something, you have to prove it.

Did you know that one time, employees at Google couldn't decide between two shades of blue so ended up testing 41 different shades? Yes, they tested 41 different shades of blue just to find out the exact color a link should have. That's impressive because it shows a fantastic mentality – that they're willing to test and test until they have the right answer.

Chances are you don't have quite the same capabilities as Google when testing your website, but you DO have the opportunity to use some incredible tools to run what are known as 'split-tests'.

Split-Tests are a test of two different versions of the same page. For example, you might test having "Book Your Tour Now!" instead of "Book Now" on your booking buttons.

This is not difficult to implement in your own site. My favorite tool is called "Visual Website Optimizer' and is located at www.vwo.com. It makes running tests simple and easy because you can test things visually instead of trying to muck around trying to edit code. It's quite literally a case of 'point and click' and that's all you need to do.

Optimizely is another popular tool.

They're best for making smaller tests – testing headlines, the words on your booking button, perhaps the order in which information is laid out. The most effective tests, however, tend to be those that make the biggest changes – for example, a complete redesign.

## Make Booking With You Damn Easy – Take Instant, PAID, Bookings Using Online Booking Software

Booking with you shouldn't be easy as pie. It should be even easier than pie.

Taking booking inquiries via email cold be the least ideal way to take bookings because of the time lapse as the visitor cools down and explores other potential options for their holiday. That's not even taking into account managing payment authorizations.

There's a million reasons why someone might want to book a tour with you at the last minute. If you don't take online bookings you're probably missing out on around 80% of these people.

So what I'm saying is this: install an online booking system already. Just do it. It doesn't even matter if you increase sales or not (and you most likely will): you'll dramatically reduce administrative overheads.

Whenever I'm on holiday, I will always use the companies that take instantaneous online bookings. Why? Fear of missing out! I'm scared that if I'm waiting for 3 days for Joe's Shark Tours to respond that Frank's Shark Tours will have sold out already! So I skip that risk and book directly with Frank.

Options include Acteavo, Rezdy, Rezgo, Checkfront,

Bookeo. Xola, TourCMS, Resmark and the list goes on.

Ecommerce is now over 20 years old. There's really no excuse in this day and age not to offer online booking capabilities.

Additional benefits of online booking systems:

1. Nearly all these systems allow for post tour follow-up. This means that you can automatically invite people to like your Facebook page and, most importantly, leave a glowing review on TripAdvisor.

2. Save yourself administrative time. All that back-and-forthing via email gets tiring, doesn't it? Let alone having to deal with booking inquiries that come in just as you're about to head out on a one week tour. You'll save yourself a lot of time and money just by investing a small amount of cash into a booking system.

3. Save on accounting costs. Given that these transactions will generally be online and automated, you'll have less difficulty integrating them with cloud-based accounting software such as Xero or Freshbooks. This will save you over the long run. Even if you don't use online accounting systems, your bookkeeper will still love you.

4. Appear more professional to people who might look to partner with you or link to you. There's no better way to appear like a small part-time company than by having a simple inquiry form. As I always say to people, imagine if you went to the website of an airline, tried to book a flight and they sent you to an inquiry form. You'd correctly think that the airline was a bit of a joke.

As websites modernize, more people expect you to take

online bookings. I know I always choose operators that will take my online booking instantly. There's nothing more frustrating for me than bumping into an inquiry form and I doubt I'm alone.

5. Vouchers. Being able to take discount vouchers and sell gift vouchers gets a whole lot easier when you're using online booking software with those capabilities.

6. Digital distribution to agents, ITOs and other companies. Self-evidently there's major benefits in being able to take bookings instantly from re-sellers without them having to go through the rigmarole of calling you up or emailing you.

7. Automated manifest management. Track your inventory automatically and with less administrative headache for you.

8. Automatically offer up-sells and cross-sells. This one feature alone can deliver a very healthy revenue bump... which leads us to the next point.

# Offer Up-sells And Cross-Sells

Q. Who is the person most likely to spend money with you?

A. The person who is already spending money with you.

For this reason, you need to offer up-sells and cross-sells. If you're a smart operator who already has implemented tour booking software, you'll probably find that you can do this without difficulty using the system that you have already chosen.

Up-sells are generally easier – and very common practice – amongst multi-day operators.

A few examples for multi-day operators:

1. Increased luxury accommodation.
2. Increased luxury transport.
3. Additional side-trips, dinners and shows.
4. Connecting tours – additional tours that you tack on before and after the tour which has already been reserved.
5. Airport transfers.
6. Insurance

None of the above should come as much of a shock and you'd most likely be familiar with

For single-day operators the most common example of up-sells are meals, airport pickups or additional activities.

Have you ever tried taking someone off a group tour and selling them on a private tour instead? If it appears that they're scared of being uncomfortable – "Does the bus have air-con?" "How many people are there total?" - you can solve that problem by offering something more exclusive.

Cross-selling involves selling other tours to the same guest. Sandemans in Europe do a great job at this on their website NewBerlinTours.com. A visitor to Berlin will book a tour with them and during the online booking process be nudged into booking one of the other day tours they have.

Now they have that rush that comes from making the purchase, that's when they're in the PERFECT position to be sold something extra. If you offer more than one tour option to your area, prepare yourself for a small bump in profits if you take the time to implement this.

## Simplify Your Pricing

Not too long ago I was looking at a New York tour operator's website.

She seemed like she had a great service but her pricing was all over the place. You basically needed a calculator and a lot of patience to figure out how much you'd have to pay if you had more than one or two people in your group.

This isn't clever by any means. A basic principle I have tried to push throughout this whole book is that people shouldn't have to work to figure out how to use your service. It should be easy and intuitive – your website, your product, your booking system, and yes, your pricing too.

Because of this, use flat pricing as much as possible. Even if your prices are a bit higher as a result, that's fine. While you may your tiered pricing as fair, many people won't - especially if it's so excessive as to become confusing.

Custom walking tour operators often have fairly complex pricing for what is the same amount of time for them. If you must charge more for larger groups, consider charging per additional head on top of a base rate. This is much easier to calculate.

## IF YOU RUN SPECIALS, HAVE A VERY GOOD REASON

One of the quickest ways to devalue the worth of your service is to run specials with no proper justification.

Try to tie specials to the season or to at least some kind of local event or recognized day, such as Valentines Day. You could easily offer regular discounts for a particular quiet day or time of the year and this would be understandable. Many day tour operators have special discounts for Tuesdays, for example. Just make sure that your discounting is explainable, not random.

This advice is based on a psychological phenomenon known as 'price anchoring'. If you show people a lower price for the same thing, they will suddenly no longer see the value in paying more – even if they were prepared to 5 minutes earlier.

## The Quickest Way To Raise Your Profits Is To Literally Raise Your Profits

There's only one genuinely good reason to be the cheapest – if you're brand new and trying to build TripAdvisor or Yelp reviews and reputation.

If you feel like you have to be the cheapest, something is going wrong, somewhere. Every discount you provide on ongoing pricing comes straight off the top of your profits! Let's say your business sells tours for $80 and the current profit per tour is around $24. If you raise your prices to $95, your profit now goes up to $39 for a 62.5% rise in profits. How much would your bookings have to drop to offset that price increase? If your bookings dropped by 38.5%, you'd still make the same profit but with a lot less work! I know I'm simplifying things somewhat here but have a look at it for your business. Play around with the maths a little bit in a spreadsheet and see what you can figure out.

The biggest lie that small business owners tell themselves is that there's some special reason or circumstance in their business which prevents them from raising prices. Please be honest: is the only reason you're not upping your prices down to fear? Do the maths on a price rise and consider the difference in PROFIT that a 10% increase in PRICE will give you. Many businesses can double their profit just from a 20% price rise.

Ironically, being the cheapest will often impact your sales negatively in any case as people wonder what is wrong with your service. Not only that, it nearly always attracts all the worst clients – those who expect something for nothing. If you feel that you can't raise prices, it's likely because you're attracting price sensitive clients who give you that kind of feedback. Not everyone is price sensitive! I used to be extremely price sensitive when I was traveling the world trying to spend as little as possible every day.

Now I just want to enjoy myself and am happy to pay the price. I know I'm not in the minority on this.

# PART 9

# DELIVERING YOUR TOUR WITH MARKETING IN MIND

Your actual service will always be one of your most powerful marketing tools. The core of all great marketing is a great product to market. If the product doesn't capture people's imagination, then it won't be easy to actually sell the thing.

In addition to having a great product which captures people's imaginations, tours need to run smoothly with the needs of both the visitor and in the business continually in mind. This part is all about making sure those needs are met.

# HOW TO BE THE TOUR GUIDE EVERYONE LOVES

We all love watching people's eyes light up when they learn something new. Unless you love boring the hell out of people, you need a way to deliver the interesting facts without putting people to sleep. Here's a few ideas to get people to love you as a guide and your team:

1. Take a personal interest in your guest. Endear yourself to your guests by having at least a small chit chat with as many as possible. Find out where they're from and how they're enjoying the local area.

It's the simple, small touches like this which spark the feeling of value that people get out of your tour. Being friendly is the foundation and taking a personal interest builds on that – it makes people feel special.

As you can imagine, I've been on many tours all around the world - I enjoy going in as a quiet observer to see how things are being done by businesses in various places. The percentage of guides who take the time to chat and take an interest in me as a person is well below 50%. What a missed opportunity to build a connection with those people.

See if you can find ways to get guests to interact with you on your tour instead of dumbly listening.

2. Tell a story. I've suffered through tours where the guide has spent hours spitting out historical data without context.

When people overload you with information you find yourself begging for the end. The exact year a big event happened is nothing compared to why and how it happened. Find the interesting nuggets and weave the information into a narrative. Make it so people can place themselves into the scenario you are building and – here's the key – really feel how the people live (or lived) in the context. If it's a nature related tour you can still build narratives – there's a story everywhere.

The fact that a building used to be important may not make it important now. It's the human angle of that building which people will find most interesting, or how it relates specifically to them. For example, with a group from India you could show them sites in your city that have historical links with their country.

3. <u>Inject a bit of humor.</u> You don't need to be a jokester but the occasional spot of humor will help. Think about it: people love laughing. Give them the thing that they love, and they will appreciate you for it.

It's not about writing a million jokes. Find the interesting and crazy stories, flesh them out and focus on them. Find the contradictions that can be amusing.

4. <u>Get dramatic!</u> You might even get your guests to close their eyes and listen to your voice as you tell the story of the place they're in and get them to feel the emotions of your characters. If talking about history, you can create an example character to talk about how someone would have lived during that time.

As you visit each place, show how your historical persona would have participated in that place and how it impacted on their society as a whole. You could even create multiple characters - one upper class, one middle class and one working class. Use this to show how each of them interacted with the same place but in dramatically different ways.

The best guides are those that help you see something in a completely new light. Be that person.

5. Master the small touches. It's the small touches that people remember and set you apart from an ordinary operator.

Bring sun block, free cold water or free snacks. This will show you as a genuine human being who cares about your guests besides just the dollars they can bring to you.

Even if you put up gigantic notices on your site and in your office saying "YOU NEED TO BRING SUN CREAM" people will always forget. If you've been in business for more than two days, you'd know this. Prepare for people's mistakes and the things that they forget, and they'll thank you for it.

Another small touch is to provide a small info booklet at the start of the trip so people can follow along with what is happening.

It's all about being a human being and doing things with love. If you're asking yourself 'how can I have the best tour possible', all this stuff will come naturally.

6. Be flexible to the needs and interests of your guest. The best tours are the ones where the guide can find points of interest to show each person so they can connect on an individual level.

## TREAT CHILDREN LIKE GOLD

If you have children, you'll know what it s like to travel with them. Sunshine, happiness and smiles 100% of the time right?

Endear yourself quickly to parents by catering to their children. Play packs, snack packs or even just a free bottle of water will go a long way.

If your tour is child friendly, take care to emphasize this in tour descriptions. Show children photos you have on your site so that prospective customers understand that you can cater to families. Even something that you may think would obviously cater to children may not be so obvious to another person.

A couple of ideas to make the tour more pleasant for kids:

1. Include them in the fun. Invite them upfront in your vehicle or to the captain's area of the ship. Kids LOVE being placed into the seats where the 'important people' normally sit. People treat children like an annoyance but if you treat them like a worthy human being you'll seriously make their day. Show them the various widgets that make up your operation. (Depending on the circumstance you may want to clear this with the parents first.)

2. Prepare fun packs – coloring, small games... You can even prepare a list of things they have to spot on the trip and if they spot all 15 they get to pick from a lucky dip. A great way to keep them engaged and enjoying themselves!

3. Bring things that parents need yet sometimes forget –

baby wipes, bottled water, tissues, sun cream, band-aids.

Put a smile on that child's face and by extension you will put a smile on the face of their parents ie. The people who paid you the money and may well leave you a glowing review the next day on TripAdvisor.

# Hiring Tour Guides? Here Are the Biggest Traits To Look For

Even if you're a one person operation, at some point in the operation of your business you're going to have to work with other guides. Here's a few criteria to select amazing guides for your business:

1. They're good people – Friendly and Empathetic. Great tour guides are the people you'd want to go have a beer with regardless of whether you were paying them.

2. They're engaged. Engaged guides take the time to learn local secrets, look after their guests, pick up a few words in important languages and are initiative takers.

3. They're professional. If you're having to upbraid someone for turning up to work late, there are massive issues there. You shouldn't have to debate basic aspects of competency with pros and you'll never hear them saying 'but that's not my job!'

4. They're great at dealing with unusual situations. If you look at the hiring processes of some of the larger tour companies in the world, they often ask potential guides what they would do in various complex situations. For example:

"A guest in your group breaks their arm and you're 3 hours away from the city you just left. You have 7 hours to reach the next place with a doctor or you can turn back. You're the only employee on site. What would you do?"

This sort of thing is definitely teachable with training. Make it a point of regular discussion among your staff to talk about what was done in a tough situation and how it can be improved.

5. They love kids. Some people just can't handle children or decide to ignore them. Do you want them leading your tours?

6. They care about the subject. Melbourne, Australia is a city I love down to the ground and it shows in every word I say about it. The same goes for Spain - Iu love every square inch. Is this just another job to your guide, or is it a topic that they can passionately discuss?

7. They're Awesome Communicators. Great guides know how to make a subject interesting to someone by understanding what it is that makes that person tick. They also know how to communicate with different personality styles in order to manage the needs of the group as a whole.

8. Bonus Point: they aspire(d) to be an actor. Great tour guides specialize in generating a positive energy and really communicating the emotion of the place they are in. If you can find someone that loves acting and hamming it up, you can give them their audience and a special day for your guests. This may not work in some niches but it's worth thinking about.

To get the most out of your guides, treat them well. In fact, if you have ever said "it's SO hard to find good people", you may want to look in the mirror! (Sorry.) Employees are the most honest mirror that you, the owner can look into.

I opened the book talking about the importance of treating

people right and I repeat it here: your guides will treat your customers like you treat them. Your whole success rests on being a great human being.

It Starts With the Job Ad

A little while back, I read this excellent piece of advice from Jason Fried of Basecamp.com:

"I hire people on the basis of the effort they put into getting the job. We don't define effort; we just ask for it. It's up to individuals to decide what it means and demonstrate it in their own way."

Ever since then, if I have needed to make an important hire this is what I do. It has not let me down once. If people make a special effort to get a job this shows hunger. Who wants an employee who thinks they're too good for the job? Not only that, but putting a good amount of effort into making a great application lets a true professional shine against the lazy layabouts.

# One Of The Biggest Causes Of Bad Reviews: Fill-In Guides

If you have the time one day, spend an afternoon browsing and reading negative reviews of other operators.

One type of complaint that repeatedly shows up on TripAdvisor is where a company has used a fill-in guide. The guest's expectation is now having to deal with your second choice and they know it. At this point they're probably feeling a bit ripped off. This is an easy situation to prepare for – you just need to be aware in advance of the damage it can cause.

For this reason, if you need to use a fill-in guide, go overboard in all other respects to ensure the happiness of the guest lest it turn into a negative review. Tell them up front what is happening, offer them their money back if they're not happy to go, and see if you can't throw in some kind of free bonus for them.

All this applies even if you think your fill-in guide of choice eats rainbows for breakfast and is the source of all light and happiness.

## USE YOUR GUESTS FOR MARKETING RESEARCH

There's little doubt that you're going to have lulls in your trips between stops where you're just making conversation with your guests. Use this time to ask your guests questions about how they go about choosing tours.

It's almost disturbing how few operators do this. You have a platinum mine of information setting right next to you – use it.

Find out what specific factors made them choose you. What has turned them off other operators. What websites they use. How they search. How they found other tours they're going on. Unless you have some kind of magic brain that knows all answers in advance, you'll learn a lot of invaluable information. One thing you'll notice is how many different ways people from other countries go about finding and booking a tour.

<u>Conduct a Formal Survey At the End of Your Tour</u>

Formal surveys are a invaluable to track the impressions of your guests and the trends in terms of how your company is improving (or not) over time.

For example, if you run a daily bus tour and every week conduct a survey of the people on the bus, you'll be able to track the figures to see whether your service is improving or if something is falling by the wayside.

Use a combination of 'rate your experience from 1-10' style questions and open ended questions such as "What would you suggest to make our tour even better?" "Were you surprised by anything today – negative or positive?"

Log this information into a spreadsheet and set monthly goals. If you find the amount of data overwhelming, is this because you're asking too many questions? If you run daily tours, you might just run the survey one day each week to reduce data overload.

This is also a great way to manage metrics to track your employees. It's a fair, honest system which you can use to manage and improve their performance over time in a transparent and fair way.

## ADD THEM TO YOUR EMAIL LIST

If you offer tours or experiences that people would come back to – such as winery tours - at the end of the tour is the best time to build your email list to generate that beautiful repeat and referral business we all love.

Obviously by this point you should have people's emails but if you don't, this is the time to mount that last, final sweep.

In your formal survey, just add the question "would you like us to let you know of further discounts or special events?"

From there you'll be able to offer them shoulder or off season discounts to fill up empty seats and the beauty of it all is that your website continues to show the same higher price. You get to reward loyal customers and fill empty seats when needed - all without compromising your brand!

## Go Social Media, Go!

Once again this applies best to those who have some level of return or referral business.

During a tour, work on getting guests to like your FB page, follow you on Instagram or perhaps even Twitter. Don't try to get them following you on ALL media channels – just the one that you have really dedicated yourself to.

Just be straight out: "Hey Josh, I have a quick favor to ask. We're trying to build our likes on Facebook so is it OK with you if you give us a like on Facebook?"

Who would ever say no to such a simple request like that? Very, very few people! The key is being directive and proactive instead of passive.

You can ask the exact same question to people about TripAdvisor reviews moments from the end "Naomi, can I ask you for the favor of leaving a TripAdvisor review after the trip? It will make a huge difference to us."

Studies have shown that if you ask people for a review and get them to confirm with a yes, you drastically increase your chances of getting it. You need to do this in addition to having an automatic system that follows up and asks for reviews straight away after the trip while they still have the memory of that promise warm in their skull.

The key here is to do it one at a time. Get the Facebook like halfway through the tour and then ask for the TripAdvisor review at the end. Extra points if you have already mentioned at some point in the tour how much TripAdvisor matters to your business.

For example:

You: "How did you find us?"

Them: "TripAdvisor"

You: "Wow. You know, TripAdvisor is so important to us it's incredible. You wouldn't believe the impact that just one or two 5 star reviews can have on our business."

If they came through Yelp, or any other site, same deal! Wherever the conversation goes at this point, don't ask them for the review. Just let it sit in their mind and then ask at the end.

Beyond this, you can use signage, incentives or just speak to people to encourage check-ins and photo uploading.

<u>Offer Free WiFi to Your Guests and Get Them Tagging</u>

One thing that many cities have been clicking to lately is that if they offer free WiFi in the city center, visitors begin to upload a mountain of photos of themselves in that location.

As a tour operator, you can take advantage of this too, depending on your offering. Even on a moving vehicle nowadays it is possible to get WiFi installed. I enjoyed WiFi for the entirety of a 5 hour bus trip recently, although with my internet addiction, this is maybe not the best thing!

By installing WiFi you can get guests to upload photos, tag themselves, and check in to your location. People are rarely alone in their interests – they'll probably have friends on their Facebook who like doing the same thing, are considering going to the same spot or who are even traveling through the same area.

## Have More Tours Available? Give Them An Incentive To Book With You Again, Right Then And There

Most tour operators in today's world have more than one tour available and there's no more perfect a prospect than someone who is already a customer and has just had a great experience with you.

Thank your guest for coming along and see if you can offer some kind of 'return special' – where if they book another day tour with you in the coming week – heck, in that moment - they can get a 10% discount.

It's common to see tour operators doing this to some extent but the key is to track your efforts week over week. What percentage of people are booking another tour? Is your incentive good enough? If you don't measure it, you can't improve it.

If you have a bunch of day tours, you could create a booklet with stamps where people receive an accumulating discount as they use more and more. Maybe if they do 3 tours, the next one is free?

# PART 10

# RELATIONSHIPS & PARTNERSHIPS

The happy thing about being a tour operator is that you'll often have a bunch of extra capacity that is pure profit if you make a sale - or zero cost for you to fill the seat for free.

Rather than tell you to print a brochure and send boxes of them to accommodation providers all over your area, let's go a little deeper and get more creative.

The key question is this: "How many local tourism business owners do you consider to be your friend?"

It could be hotel operators or local booking agents but the answer to that question will be one of the biggest determinants of your success in this space.

## Do A Free Tour For Local Tourism Operators, Hotel Owners Or Hostel Owners

At least once a year, I'd recommend dedicating a day (or three) to taking out owners of other local tourism businesses and their employees during the off-season.

Get them to come on the actual tour with you and along the way you can build relationships.

It's easy for them to know vaguely who you are, but that doesn't help. If people running complementary businesses can have a genuine taste of your service, you'll stay in their mind forever – and they'll be much more likely to recommend you to their own customers.

It's a great way to compare marketing notes with people who are in a similar industry to you. For something so small, there's just no way it can hurt.

Invite hotel and hostel owners, employees from the local tourism association or even owners of non-competing tour companies and have a blast.

*Matthew Newton*

# CREATE A TOURISM TEAM IN YOUR AREA

Getting other people to sell your tours may not work in many cases.

What about banding with other tour operators to create joint promotional material? This way, you create the 'authority piece' – the brochure that all people get handed when they check in at hotels and hostels all around your region. Your instinct may be to go it alone, but let's be realistic – as an operator, how much is your brochure going to stand out against the 100 others that are already sitting around in the hotel lobby?

For example, in Australia's Yarra Valley a group of brewery operators joined together to create the "Yarra Valley Cider and Ale Trail." It's been incredibly popular and means that many people will spend a day or two completing the trail by going to every business listed on it. So simple, yet devastatingly effective.

You could make it so each operator or provider offers a standard discount to guests. It gives the material higher value and makes it so there's only one standard printed piece going around rather than 20.

Incentivize things further by rewarding travelers for using multiple services. For example, operators could stamp on the name of their business as someone goes through – the more stamps, the bigger the discount.

Or, you could just create a basic tourism guide to your area that has various providers listed. If it's genuinely useful, you and your tourism team will be able to heavily distribute it to accommodation providers and they'll actually use it.

You won't even need to create special discounts if you can create a narrative which makes sense. Returning to the "Cider and Ale Trail" mentioned earlier, they've created something which people want to complete without having to be bribed into doing it by simple discounts.

Earlier in the book, I discussed the fear of missing out and its powerful sub-currents. 'Completing the set' is just one demonstration of this fear – people don't want to leave an area without feeling they have done 'everything there is to do'.

## BUILDING RELATIONSHIPS WITH ACCOMMODATION PROVIDERS

Whenever you go to a hotel or hostel you'll most likely notice a large amount of ignored brochures sitting around. Here's the tips to avoid your marketing materials being lumped in with a bunch of other paper:

1. Make sure to actually build a relationship. It's rude to just send brochures to an accommodation provider without any accompanying relationship building. "Oh hey, I can't be bothered talking to you, but please sell my business."

2. Try posters. I know I pay a lot more attention to posters than to brochures.

3. Make your printed marketing a different shape, size and material. Avoid as many of the 'typical boring brochure' design features and you'll come a long way. Make a brochure that looks just like the rest and guess what - you'll be treated just like the rest.

4. Focus on a small quantity of high quality relationships. This will serve you much better in the long run than a scatter-gun 'gotta have em all' approach. 5 successful accommodation provider relationships will deliver you much more rewards than 40 mediocre ones.

5. Stay in touch with them. Like their Facebook Pages and respond to their posts. Follow them on Twitter re-tweet their tweets to your followers. Be their friend!

6. The best way to make people love you: send them business. Send business and send lots of it. Yes, it's hard

to refer people to accommodation while they are on a day tour as they will already have a place to stay. That being said, when someone books with you 4 weeks in advance, why don't you make the recommendation then? It could be part of your 'thank-you' email – if you're not using that thank-you email to make up-sells and cross-sells, at the least recommend a trusted local hotel.

7. Make your standard pick-up points accommodation providers (if they aren't already). Go deep with several accommodation providers and make their hotels pick-up points for your tours. This way you can't help but be on their minds – and that of all their staff.

8. Leave the best impression possible. Did you know that when a hotel refers someone to a tour and they have a bad time, often guests will leave a negative review of the hotel? This means that accommodation providers are very hesitant to build referral relationships with tour businesses - it could easily hurt their own business. If you can point to pre-existing successful relationships, your positive reviews on social media, your insurance and your qualifications you'll be much more likely to convince them.

## ALLOW LOCAL ACCOMMODATION TO SELL YOUR TOURS

Accommodation owners and staff are always being peppered with questions as to ideas for things to do.

What if they were able to sell your tours on your behalf? Personally, the reception front desk is the first place I always go when I arrive in a destination and have a bit of time to kill in the next few days. One thing I really like seeing is when a hotel has a deal with a tour provider where they sell the tours directly to you. As a guest, the reason I love this is because it saves me so much time – even if it costs a bit more.

The hotel owner or concierge wins because they get a commission and tour operators win because they get a bunch more clients that they never would have had.

Be aware that accommodation providers are much more likely to book with you on an ongoing basis if you make it super simple for them. Gone are the days of the ticket book where they have to fill out a ticket with a carbon copy. It will work much better for you and for them to have an online portal where they can just book directly with you, no hassles.

How would you do this? Simple – most major tour operator software systems allow for you to set up agents or re-sellers so that they can re-sell your products and make the booking on the spot without any hand-holding or back-and-forthing with your team about availability.

*Sell More Tours*

It's not legal in many jurisdictions for accommodation providers to do this without a license so tread carefully with this one. Check with your local tourism association if it is permitted in your area for hostels/hotels to re-sell your packages.

Offer appropriate commissions and ensure that front desk staff get a cut of it. They're much more likely to go through the hassle of booking a tour with you if they get a reward!

## Level Up – Do You Have Packages For Sale With Other Complementary Businesses?

Let's get serious here.

We all know that tour operators often bring a significant amount of business to places like local hotels.

What if we made that a two-way street – do you think you could create joint packages with accommodation providers? What if the hotels themselves could sell your packages?

For example, they could sell 'Romantic Weekend' packages that include a winery tour with your company. 'Active Weekend' packages could include white water rafting trips (and so on).

The only way this sort of thing can ever happen is if you get off your butt and make it happen!

Here's a few ideas to make partnerships successful:

1. You need a genuine, ongoing relationship. It's too easy to make an alliance over a handshake. Both parties need to be committed to making it work. It's best to do this kind of thing with someone you already have a pre-existing relationship with.

2. Mutual effort. Both of you need to give the packages prominence on your sites and make genuine efforts to sell them.

3. Give the packages a special angle. You can tie them to sentiments such as the Romantic Weekend concept above

but also local events such as major horse races.

**4. Get your local DMO or tourism association on this.** You'll find that your tourism association may well happily feature special packages like this in their own materials. If a few local businesses have teamed up, it makes it easy for them to justify selecting your promotion. Get them on board and who knows what magic could happen.

**5. Get bloggers to come out and experience your co-branded package.** I've talked previously in this book about working with bloggers . If you're struggling to get bloggers out for a free tour just with you (which is highly unlikely), then you'll find it easier to get them on board for full experience packages. Especially higher profile bloggers, who often look down their noses at smaller experiences, will find themselves more likely to respond to packages that follow more of a narrative.

The key thing here that you don't sit around and wait for your tourism association to get things happening for you. Take the initiative to build relationships and hustle up some business. Your bank account will be grateful!

## GET REFERRALS FROM OTHER BUSINESSES? TAKE THE TIME TO LET THEM KNOW

The number one reason other owners in the area will stop referring clients to your business is that they hear bad things from the people they send on your tours. The second biggest reason is that they never hear anything back after the referral happens! That moment following the referral is key to your relationship – they've just sent you a money-spending client and your reaction in this moment should not be silence.

If you were continuously sending paying customers to a certain operator or hotel and NEVER heard back about it, you'd stop too! Ungrateful so-and-sos.

For this reason, the best way to encourage continued referrals is to keep the referrer posted as to what's going on – even if that person doesn't end up coming with you.

You don't need to go overboard in your appreciation. If someone is sending you an absolute mountain of business, obviously in that scenario a gift could well be appropriate. Other than that, a simple 'thank-you' goes a long way.

Either way, every single time a small business sends you business for the first time, write them a thank-you note. Hand-written thank-you cards are rare which makes them memorable... and the number one most important step to keep getting referrals is that they actually remember who you are! Not only that, but gratitude is a great practice not just for your bank account but for your overall well-being.

## An Alternative To Sponsoring Bloggers And Online Guides: Make Them Affiliates

A new option now available to customers of some tour operator software packages is to set up websites and bloggers as affiliates.

An affiliate is someone that places ads and links to your website on their site and receives a commission on every booking that takes place.

A few tips on managing affiliates:

1. The key here is not to treat affiliates as a 'set and forget' relationship – this would be an enormous mistake. As with all business partnerships, for the bookings to happen you need the relationship first and the business will come next.

2. Pay generous rates to affiliates to give them an incentive to sell and push your tours. Always remember that you would never have gotten the client if it weren't for them.

3. Work alongside them to provide marketing collateral to promote your service. Give them something to talk about.

4. Work with them on larger promotions and group trips. You could create a special day for their website where their website visitors book with you as a community. Everyone wins!

## Tips For Making The Most Of Online Travel Agents (OTAs).

OTAs are an attractive proposition for many tour operators. No wonder - it's like having an additional sales force working for you without you having to lift a finger! In terms of how many bookings OTAs bring in, you may find yourself disappointed if you're expecting them to carry your business. Treat the clients that come through these systems as the 'cream' on top of your ordinary profits but not as the bread and butter.

To get the most out of your OTA relationships, you need to have nailed the core aspects of your marketing. Having an amazing looking website with great copy, video and photography will show that you're an operator who values excellence and wants to work hard to sell your tours.

If accepted by these websites – Viator, Expedia and friends – you'll be lumped in with a whole bunch of tour options. Don't expect these sites to do a whole amount to help you. Instead, do it yourself.

Analyze how they are ranking the tour operators in your area and spend some time making sure your listing stands out. This is where having great copy and imagery comes in handy once again – eyes are always sucked in by beautiful photos.

A major headache, however, of dealing with OTAs is that they will 'own the client' – they'll get a little stroppy with you if you try to sell the guest to go on another tour. It's something that comes in the terms and conditions but it's hard to imagine how they enforce that particular rule. You do need to be wary of it though.

Check with your tour operator software provider about how well they are able to integrate with these platforms. To avoid overbooking, you may need to dedicate some space on each trip to these giants which could then mean that you experience lost sales.

Keep in mind TripAdvisor and Yelp – annoying just one customer enough to receive a one star review can kick your business way down in the rankings and do hurtful damage to your bottom line. If they come from an OTA, still treat them well!

## TOUR GUIDES, SHOULD YOU GET YOURSELF LISTED ON ALL THE TOUR GUIDE MARKETPLACES?

Nowadays it seems like a disturbing amount of techies are rolling out of bed one day and deciding that their dream in life is to create a tour guide marketplace. We're not talking portals for tour companies like Viator (which are also in abundance) – we're talking about the 'local guide' type of websites that only let customers book experiences with individual guides.

The success of Airbnb in the accommodation space has led many to have a stab at creating similar websites for tour guides – including Airbnb themselves.

This has led to a highly fragmented market on the internet with many places you can get listed. Why not spend an afternoon putting yourself up on all of them? If one of them explodes, you will gain an advantage by being there earlier. It's nearly always the first people arriving onto a platform that end up being the biggest winners.

The issues begin where the websites have a live availability calendar. In that case, start-ups such as Rezdy allow you to show the same availability on your website as you show to everybody and over time, are adding access to more and more activity websites which actually generate business for you.

Examples include Zerve.com, Vayable.com, GetYourGuide.com, TourRadar.com, Yetti.com, Rent-A-Guide.com and

ToursByLocals.com.

Some of the above mentioned sites are – at least at the start of 2015 – picking up steam. There's also potential for the links that can come from this sites, plus if you have a Google My Business listing you get some benefit from having either your phone number or address listed (see if you can squeeze it past their moderators.)

# PART 11

# BONUS TIPS

## Make This Someone's Job

It's hard to manage a proper marketing campaign if you're relying on yourself to do it and run tours at the same time. Your hands are full doing too many other things to have a proper crack.

Beyond hiring an agency, the smartest option is to make it someone's job. If you don't yet have an employee you can hire someone to help you on a part time basis spending too much. Investing in someone to help you with marketing is one of the easiest ways to get an actual return on investment and you'll thank yourself over time.

You could even hire a marketing student from a local university. Getting genuine marketing experience is invaluable to students who are desperately clawing to find an advantage which will help them land a job once they're out in the real world looking. This way, you get affordable help and they get valuable lines on their resumé.

As to their training, just hand them this book and tell them to start reading!

## BE A TOURIST: GO ON OTHER TOURS

Pass too much time in your own echo chamber and you'll go deaf.

Go on tours run by other operators, especially ones that are successful. It will help you rejuvenate your mind and find new inspiration for improvements and ideas.

Sit and learn from them. Observe what they're doing because possibly even they don't know what their special sauce is. Sometimes the smallest things make the biggest difference.

From time to time, you'll have forehead smacking 'OF COURSE!' or 'How did I forget that?' moments.

## How Many Languages Can Your Team Speak?

When building your time and making hires, try to find people who can speak a second or third language.

This can greatly expand your field of operations. You can now create a version of your website for that language.

Chinese is the classic example but there's many more options you could consider. The Chinese market is exploding and many are rushing to make sales to this market. However, most Chinese guests book their entire trips through ITOs in China – who will use local Chinese operators in your city.

Once you throw up a translated version of your site, that this is not the end of things. As we have seen already here, 'crossing your fingers and hoping' doesn't yet qualify as a first-rate marketing strategy (when it does, I'll update the book!)

If you don't speak the particular language that you're offering, a staff member will need to assist you in making sure your business is listed on all the correct websites which would naturally push business towards you. Chinese visitors don't spend a huge amount of time on TripAdvisor, for example.

Unfortunately, most tourism operators tend to find that their multilingual efforts falter - it's because they're not jumping in with two feet! If you dedicate genuine time and resources to this, you'll come out as the winner and remember – not all tourists in the world are Chinese. There's still a load of

Europeans who speak English but would prefer to tour in their own language.

# Consider Variable Pricing To Maximize Profits

Many operators tend to implement a high-season – low-season pricing model.

Some go further and implement a high-season – low-season – shoulder-season pricing system.

Why not dial this up even further? There'll be certain periods or days when you know you're guaranteed to book out. Why not create special pricing for those specific days?

If you're concerned about ripping people off or confusing people with varied pricing, why not create specific custom offers for those days, events or periods which include services or luxuries. This means you make it impossible to do a specific apples-to-apples comparison in terms of pricing and allows you to avoid the confusion that can come from listing the same event for multiple different prices in the same week.

That way, you have a special tour for a special event and everyone is happy.

Some providers of tour booking software allow you to run what is more or less an airline model, where prices go up and down automatically depending on how a particular tour is selling. This kind of system has been enormously effective for airlines. Why shouldn't it be effective for you? At the least, it's worth looking into.

I know that I said earlier in the book that you should keep your pricing simple. Am I contradicting myself? I don't think so. If at the time of viewing pricing is relatively simple, then this is fine. It might be complicated to you as you watch your system push prices up and down, but if I log in and see $89 as a price (without knowing that your day tour cost $88 the day before), then that's fine.

## IF A CLIENT WANTS A REFUND, FOR ANY REASON, NO MATTER HOW STUPID, GIVE IT TO THEM!

One of the most difficult things to do as a business owner is to give refunds to people who are idiots. When someone is being an entitled jerk - when they haven't read your website OR your follow-up emails and now they blame you – it can be hard to be nice.

That's why when they ask for a refund you want to tell them where to shove it. Here's the problem of today's day and age: there's a good chance they have a TripAdvisor account and they're ready to use it. Maybe as a bonus they'll even slam you on Yelp.

I've seen hundreds upon hundreds of negative reviews and in my estimation, around 50-60% of them could have been avoided if the operator just offered a refund without fighting the guest. Refunds might cost you $100, $150, $300 but the negative review can cost you SO much more.

Case in point: I recently found a tour operator who received 4 negative reviews from the same group all because he was a bit vague on the phone about additional costs. The group was so annoyed with their experience that they sat down one by one and destroyed his rating. That business had shut down by the time I discovered it. Ouch.

It was impossible from reading the reviews to know who was in the right but there was one undisputed fact that both parties agreed on – that the group left almost as soon as arriving. This means that the tour operator let someone walk away AND kept their money. This is absolutely nuts. I don't care if you're in the right – if someone is CONVINCED that you told them something, and it's looking like a showdown, just give them what they want.

In this particular case, the group was annoyed that a certain add-on wasn't included in the price. That business could have saved themselves major heartache by just being flexible in mentality and keeping their eyes on the long game. I doubt that they shut down just because of 4 bad reviews – although if you depend too much in TripAdvisor, anything is possible – rather that this outcome was a symptom of the mentality of the owner.

The principle of the matter says that you should tell them where to go. The economics of the matter says 'swallow your pride.'

## Follow The Competition To Your Death

In my experience, the number one reason that tourism businesses begin to spend money on marketing is because they see a competitor doing it. This comes back to the 'fear of missing out' that I mentioned much earlier in the book – you're worried that they're out there getting business that you're missing out on.

It's perfectly understandable to do this but just be careful of the ramifications. How much will you copy your competition? How much are you going to imitate? How many sales will you make blindly following someone?

Most importantly: why did you wait for them to move before you took action?

Create your own marketing plan. Implement it. Test techniques and methods. It may well be worth testing out a few marketing tactics that your competitor is using, but you need to have clear reasons why that would be and how much effect it would be having.

## Marketing Almost Never Works.... On The First Try

The internet is littered with the bodies of websites who started a blog and wrote 5 posts. Websites who spent $100 on Google Adwords and had it fail on them. Those who tried one press release and got no response.

It's incredibly rare for marketing campaigns to succeed right off the bat. It's all about re-assessing, refining and then stepping up again to the plate!

It almost feels redundantly obvious to say this, but there actually are people with successful blogs, Adwords campaigns and PR campaigns out there. This means very often that it's not blogging or Adwords which were the poor decisions that caused you to waste marketing money – the poor decision lay elsewhere. Most likely, it was just a failure of persistent execution as opposed to anything else that caused your marketing to bomb.

With nearly all marketing strategies, the key is to iterate – keep on getting better, learning, executing, learning, executing, learning, executing.

Often you'll find that improvements in one place will help you elsewhere. For example, if you follow all the tips above about how to build a website to make sales, you could find that your Google Adwords campaigns could suddenly become a whole lot more profitable.

## Wrapping Up

There's many tactics listed in this book. All of them have worked for someone at some point. As you finish reading this, I just want you to remember the framework of principles that I outlined at the start of the book:

Be a great friend to your market. Know your difference and communicate this to your herd. Persist through the marketing initiatives that don't work on the first shot. Take action every single day. Focus on only a few channels at any one time.

Email me at matthew@tourismtiger with your thoughts and feedback on this book.

Follow us – Facebook.com/tourismtiger & Twitter at @hitourismtiger

At TourismTiger we do websites and online marketing for local tourism businesses. Check us out to see if we're a good fit.

Here's to your success!

Matthew.

PS. Subscribe to our videos at tourismtiger.com/videos/

PPS. Don't forget to sign up for free updates to this book at tourismtiger.com/bookupdates/

Printed in Poland
by Amazon Fulfillment
Poland Sp. z o.o., Wrocław